Undulations

A Journey on the Appalachian Trail

Undulations

A Journey on the Appalachian Trail

By Karen Thompson
a.k.a. "Dances With Scarf"

Undulations: A Journey on the Appalachian Trail

ISBN 978-0-615-33838-5
$20.00

Printed in the United States of America by Innovative Business Concepts, Inc., Russell Springs, KY

For additional copies contact Karen Thompson at www.karenonthetrail.com.

Photo Credits: All photos are the author's.
Cover painting: Sunrise from Clingman's Dome, Tennessee (highest point on the entire Appalachian Trail) by Butch Hodgkins

This Book is Dedicated to the Creator

Thanking God at Journey's End on Mt. Katahdin,
Maine

"i thank God for most this amazing day for the
leaping greenly spirits of trees and a blue true
dream of sky-for everything which is natural
which is infinite which is yes."

e.e. cummings

Acknowledgements

"To live the heroic life is to live the individual adventure."
Joseph Campbell

Thank you, Barbara Quinn or as I fondly call you "Nails" (it is customary on the Appalachian Trail to take on a nickname or trail name). You are truly one of the greatest gifts the AT gave me.

"Nails" and "Dances with Scarf" Giddy on Katahdin's Tableland

I have infinite love and appreciation for my children- Ezra Muir, Chenoa Joia and Dustin Chad; they were with me every step and breath of the trail. Their unfailing support and love surround me always. The truth be known- they are my greatest dream come true and my utmost and continuous life adventure is that of being their momma.

I lovingly thank my Mom for life, strong legs, heart and her thoughtful food boxes.

I am grateful to my Daddy for his watchful and loving eyes from Heaven.

Wayne and Judy, my unconditional loving brother and sister-in-heart, what can I say? You both are truly amazing and exemplify the purest model of Christian love I have ever known. An extra thanks for the awesome website- www.karenonthetrail.com - you created and kept current while I was on the trail.

There are so many others to thank:

Rich Quinn "Mr. Nails" for his tremendous care of "Nails" and me on the trail and his lifelong friendship

Ellen Casey for my food boxes, surprise goodies, friendship and encouragement

Bill Cooke or "Cooker Hiker" for his tireless trail support

The Barna family for meeting me on the trail twice for needed R&R's

Suzanne Jessamyn for her surprise and fun mail drop boxes (near May Day, one had temporary flower and butterfly tattoos in it to lighten my day) and her cherished forever friendship

    Carol Yirka for yummy Easter goodies sent, her continually supportive and wise counsel and love given to me over the miles and years

    Arlene Foster for her constant friendship, prayers and support

    Bert Emmerson or "Wildcat" for being a true gentleman on the trail

    Howard Duncan for truly sharing in understanding this dream, especially in the early dreaming stages

    and for the many folks unnamed – in trail towns, hostels, churches, post offices, on the highway, friends and family at home – that through their kindness and support made my path smoother and richer. Thank you.

Contents

"To walk. To see. To see what you see."
Benton MacKaye

x

Introduction

*"Climb the mountains and get their good tidings.
Nature's peace will flow into you as sunshine flows
into trees. The winds will blow their own freshness
into you and the storms their energy while cares
will drop off like autumn leaves."*

John Muir – 1911

Undulation is defined, at its simplest, as a graceful rising and falling motion. I feel this is a perfect holistic definition of the experience of hiking from Georgia to Maine on the Appalachian Trail. Walking a long distance trail is a constant roller coaster of physical, mental, emotional and spiritual ups and downs and the ensuing challenge of striving to flow elegantly with the ride. The journey is one of rolling contrasts as well – an ebb and flow of hot/cold, wet/dry, euphoria/blues, weary/fresh, weak/strong, deprivation/fullness, agony/ecstasy, monotony/absorption, thirst/saturation and infinite more opposites. The task of maneuvering these undulations and poles with poise is a constant, though somewhat unconscious, greater purpose of an AT hiker. The dual taskmasters are the pull of "home" each evening (generally three-sided rough wood shelters or camping spots distributed along the trail in respectable daily hiking intervals) and the extraordinary lure of that last up. The final mountain and northern terminus of the AT in Maine is Mt. Katahdin, the name meaning "greatest mountain." Though this greatest peak is, from the beginning or southern terminus of the trail at Springer Mountain, Georgia, literally thousands of miles ahead, never is

1

it far from mind nor boots. For 2174.1 miles, 14 states, 177 days and 5,000,000+ steps I walked the Appalachian Trail, sometimes as a stumblebum, other times as an eloquent dancer, one step at a time – up, down, up, down, up and down walking my dream.

The Possible Dream

"Sometimes I've believed as many as six impossible things before breakfast."
Queen in "Alice in Wonderland"
Lewis Carroll

Hiking the entire Appalachian Trail from Georgia to Maine has always been a dream of mine. It is number nine of "one hundred things to do in my life" – a list written in a ten-year old dreamy blue-eyed girl's diary. I don't remember its particular inception; I have no story of holding my father's hand at seven asking innocently, "What does that white blaze on the tree mean, Daddy?" as we hiked in the Smokies. I have no recollection of first even reading or hearing about the trail and saying in my heart and soul, "I am going to do that some day!" As a young impressionable person, my heroes or heroines were not 2000 milers I worshiped and planned to literally walk in their footsteps.

I certainly now though greatly admire the folks that built and walked the trail before me. Massachusetts regional planner Benton MacKaye, whose vision to preserve a wilderness belt along the Appalachian crest (first proposed in 1921 and opening as a continuous trail in 1937) gave us this remarkable footpath. The trail was designed and constructed by volunteer hiking clubs coordinated by the newly formed Appalachian Trail Conservancy, also volunteer-based and nonprofit. Myron Avery, ATC chairman from 1931 to 1952, was the first person to complete the

3

entire trail, doing it in sections. A legend on the trail, Emma "Grandma" Gatewood, is reputed to be the first woman to walk the complete trail at age 65 in 1955. Earl Shaffer was the first thru-hiker which is defined as finishing the whole trail in one season. He actually did it thrice; in 1948 he completed a northbound thru-hike, a southbound thru-hike in 1965 and to celebrate his fiftieth anniversary of the first hike he completed a third northbound thru-hike at the age of 79. I can understand why his trail name is "Crazy One!"

The 1968 National Trails System Act made the AT a linear national park. The National Park Service now protects, preserves and maintains this public footpath in a unique partnership with the ATC, USDA Forest Service and the incredible volunteer-based trail-maintaining clubs along the corridor of the AT, so that hikers can continue to enjoy this one-of-a-kind park. An inspiring blind man, Bill Irwin, thru-hiked the entire trail in 1990 with his guide dog, Orient, writing about his journey in a book titled Blind Courage. A young couple, the woman pregnant, birthed a healthy baby girl just weeks after finishing the trail, naming her Georgia Maine. There are many others unnamed here who have walked before me, but at the age of ten I had never heard their names.

No, truly, I just can't cite a time in my life when I didn't hear the call of this trail and hold this dream close. Maybe my mother, carrying me in her womb, read about the AT or saw a documentary on it and there floating in fertile magical water, the dream seed was planted in my soul. Perhaps it is a higher power destiny for my life. More than likely though it

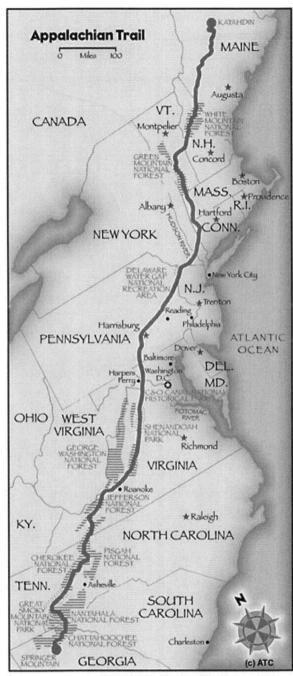

The Appalachian Trail from Maine to Georgia

is simply a human dream, nurtured over my life so that it did not perish, waiting for its season of fruition.

Harvest Time

*"Whatever you can do or dream you can, begin it.
Boldness has genius, power and magic in it."*

Goethe

As I was happily making a dent on the other ninety-nine entries in that diary, my AT dream, gently covered in a sea of "not yet," would bob to the surface periodically to breathe. During a hike with my children or in a bookstore travel section it would swell my heart with its inhalation. The current of time at last drew it close to shore and I could feel the tickle of the ocean wave that would wash my feet onto the rock at Springer Mountain, Georgia. The receding fizzy foam will expose the first white blaze of the Appalachian Trail and my long awaited vision will commence.

What does one feel when a long dreamed for aspiration surfaces? I felt elation, apprehension, anticipation, fear, excitement, deep breaths and wide smiles. "Yes!" was immediately followed by, "Can I do it?" Will the journey live up to the expectations of a lifetime of envisioning it? As the dream bobbed closer and closer to the shore, AT maps appeared on my bedroom and bathroom walls, affirmations on post-it-notes stuck on the beginning point. I read everything I could find on the trail. I talked about it to anyone and everyone who had the patience to humor me. I ignored eyes and words that discouraged and gratefully soaked up positive expressions.

Three months before the hike I started an in-depth conditioning period. Though I try to live a lifestyle conducive to holistic health, I wanted to do all I could do to insure vitality and happiness on this longest hike of my life. I began intense reading, praying and meditating about my coming pilgrimage. For one month I hiked with my loaded pack (35-40 pounds) every other day for 5-10 miles per day; with one overnight trip that month. The next month I increased my mileage per day to 10-15, adding a second overnight trip. Month three I went on four three day backpacking trips covering 16-20 miles per day. I am fortunate in that I have Big South Fork National River and Recreation Area and Daniel Boone National Forest twenty minutes from my home. The Great Smoky Mountains National Park is just a four hour drive away, so I had plenty of playgrounds to romp in.

I remember one particular conditioning hike day when I woke up at home to a cold and dreary rain. I almost talked myself out of going that day; I mean I didn't have to, right? But discipline won out and the morning hike was horrible as I suspected it would be. "Why am I doing this?" I moaned to myself. As I hiked, the temperature plummeted and the yucky rain changed to a peaceful snowfall, gracefully decorating the hemlock, pines and rhododendrons. It was so beautiful; I knew this is how the trail would be – a day so difficult I just can't go on, then a gift will appear to remind me of the reasons I am doing this.

I began the planning and packing of my re-supply boxes which would be mailed to me in towns near the trail corridor by my friend Ellen, who I dubbed with the trail name "Umbilical Cord," and by my mom. It is a huge responsibility to be a thru-hiker's re-supply person. They are truly an umbilical cord - supplying life food, hygienic items, maps, news from home, replacement gear when needed, first aid stock and film. They are our main link to survival, home, safety and our "other life." They virtually walk the trail with you. Ellen and Mom were both incredible; my boxes were always at the post office waiting for me. They went over-and-beyond the call of duty by putting extra treats and surprises in my box. Letters and emails from other people, thoughtful gifts, creative food extras and cards of encouragement put a bounce in my step on the trail.

I will take a bit of an excursion here to mention one particular mail drop box from Ellen that contained a mysterious blue-black liquid in a small plastic bottle. One sniff that day, sitting outside a post office in Virginia with my mail drop supplies spread out all around me like spoils from a raid, and a mischievous smile decorated my face - her homemade blackberry brandy! I would save this for a pertinent occasion!

A few days later, I came into an over-full shelter late, wet, cold, physically and mentally beat from a difficult day hiking in rain and cold. The day got even more arduous with the sinking realization that there was no room in the inn and I had to set up my tent in the rain, cook supper in the rain and go fill my water containers in the rain at a spring 300 slippery feet downhill. Then I remembered the magic liquid and asked myself, "Opportune time for a night-cap when all the chores were done? You betcha!" Their bodies already cozy in the full and dry shelter, I set my fellow hikers' minds into confusion and wonderment as they watched me do my evening tasks in the rain with a husky smirk spread all over my face!

My responsibilities finally completed and at last warm and dry laying in my tent, I listened to the rain and sipped on that delicious sweet brandy. A mind-altering state for my situation was created with that warm magic in my belly; actually my outlook for the evening shifted at first thought, before even a drop touched my leering lips. I didn't care about the added risk of bears I took with taking food into my tent. That night I had no worries. It was the one time I didn't share my goodies from home, as was common when hikers got special treats in our mail drop boxes; sorry.

Back to Ellen and Mom - they would mail my boxes to me at appointed times and places to My Name, AT Thru-hiker, General Delivery, AT Trail Town, USA. My kitchen table was piled to the ceiling with zip lock bags of nuts, berries, granola (I made four large size black garbage bags of homemade granola) and every dried meal concoction you can imagine - even tofu! My dehydrator magically turned wet spoils into dry keeps. Toiletries, vitamins and first aid items placed in baggies in the amounts I would need for one to two weeks were filled and labeled.

Another digression here; I apologize for my jumpiness. Applicable tales need to be told. The Christmas prior to my departure date of February, I asked my family to give me gifts of needed items for my six-month hike on the AT. My niece, Andrea, creatively, individually and painstakingly wrapped 24 tiny tubes of toothpaste for my gift; what a unique and great idea! Well it gets even funner! Ellen or Mom would put one of these in each of my mail drop boxes. I told them not to unwrap them so I could continue to get the pleasure of opening these small gifts on the trail. One day, after eating out, getting our boxes at the post office, eating out (again) and buying other supplies in the trail town, "Nails," "Mountain Man," "Camel" and I headed out of town together back to the trail. That May evening, sitting at the shelter, "Camel" moans, "Oh, man, I forgot to get toothpaste in town and I am totally out!" I still had some left from a tube from the last supply box, so I had not opened the new Christmas wrapped box of tooth- paste. Walking up to "Camel" holding out the gift, I said, "Merry Christmas, 'Camel'." Opening it with a perplexed look on his face, he said, "But how...."

Also in the mailed boxes were film, journal pages, torn-out sections of the AT guides (we try not to carry ANY unnecessary weight) and current maps. I

"Mountain Man," "Camel," "Scarf" and "Nails" in Virginia

have heard of some hikers even taking off the labels in their clothing, cutting off the end of their toothbrush or drilling holes in the handle to lighten up their pack weight. Carrying paper and pen for journaling was a bit of a luxury, but it was important to me to record this special journey as it was happening so the feelings and impressions would be fresh and pure. Meticulously, the maps and guides were put in the correct dated drop mail box for the time on the trail they each would be needed. The pile of "stuff" on my table and living room floor that at first had looked complicated and impossible to organize, began to have order. It was impossible to think, though, that I could carry all this plunder to Maine! One step at a time, I reminded myself.

Oh how I anticipated that first footstep! My long-denied soul dream ached for release; my hiking boot clad feet were itching to walk this trail. I laugh at the imagery that arises at these words for I am an experienced enough hiker at the onset to know the reality I will live on the trail. I will barter back and forth these spiritual aches and itches for physical pangs and twinges; dreamy intangibles will be interspersed with throbbing tangibles. So with open eyes, a positive heart and undeniable antsy feet, I set a departure date - February 29, 2004 - Leap Day - a fitting day to begin a hop from Georgia to Maine I thought (and I figured I could well use the extra day in the year). Oops- now I was committed! Now it was real; now it was going to happen!

First Steps

"The journey of a thousand miles begins with one step."
Lao Tzu

My family - my daughter, mom, brother and sister-in-heart - ceremoniously escorted me to Springer Mountain, Georgia, on February 29, 2004. The night before, we stayed at the Amicalola Falls Lodge, eating my "last big supper" and then my "last big breakfast." I was excitingly eying other potential hikers in the dining room. My beautiful family hiked with me to the top of Springer Mountain where we circled that first white AT blaze holding hands and hearts and my

My Wonderful Family Send Off

First White Blaze on Springer Mountain, Georgia

daughter said a touching prayer. After this incredible send-off I tearfully walked into the woods, waving goodbye to my family as doubts battled with elation for room in my gut. What may be - I had begun my journey.

A fun and interesting tradition on the Appalachian Trail is the adoption of a trail name. The stories, meanings, intents, visions and humor behind a trail name are infinite. Some hikers give themselves a name before they began their trek - a name that has personal meaning to them. Others let a name conspire on or from experiences once they get on the trail. Mine happened in the latter way on my first evening of hiking the AT.

I was quite giddy that whole first day. The joy, which had won the skirmish by the way, could not be wiped from my face despite my aching feet and back yelling that I had nothing to smile about as they adjusted to their new role of Sherpa (one lady gave herself that trail name). My first night's home on the trail was Hawk Mountain Shelter, shared with "Nuffy," a girl from Australia who had heard about the AT from reading Bill Bryson's book <u>A Walk in the Woods</u>, three young guys from Georgia, Josh (later named "Happy Feet") from Tennessee and a gal, a delight in small dosages, living up to her name "Giggles." What a wonderful "surrogate family" for my first night! After cooking my special first trail dinner of peace-shaped pasta and cheese sauce, laying out my sleeping pad and bag on the wooden floor, hanging my food bag from a tree, filling up and treating water for my bottles, I sat on the edge of the shelter floor watching the night fall.

Contemplating the wonder-full day, I realized this is not just a weekend backpack trip; I have begun my lifelong dream of hiking the Appalachian Trail! I could not contain the rapture in that moment and tired though my body was, my spirit was stronger. I jumped up, grabbed the sweat soaked scarf off my head and danced around in front of the shelter waving my green paisley "flag" exuberantly, merrily chanting, "I am doing it! I am hiking the AT!" Laughing at my antics, "Nuffy" dubbed me "Dances with Scarf" and it stuck. It did get shortened by most to just "Scarf." That infamous dancing scarf, tattered and soiled, did not retire till her final dance on Mt. Katahdin in Maine on September 18, 2007.

But I am getting way ahead of my story and my "first steps." Day three began and ended, as many

Dancing with Scarf

did in late winter and early springtime, with rain. Packing up in the morning to the sound of rain is the best de-motivator there is - ugh!!! Those first few moments of waking to a soothing sonata of rain on the roof, tender drippings of water off the trees and the wholesome smell of a cleansed forest with its moist rich soil is tranquil and fragrant with hope. But serene optimism quickly turns to dank irritation as the challenges involved with hiking in rain seep in to dampen the day's outlook. Putting rain gear on myself and my pack, saying goodbye to dry boots and leaving a nice dry shelter is just not right.

   That third day it rained without a break. It is hard to stop for rests, water, food and views (though they are disappointedly hidden anyway) when it is raining. A shivery chill sets in quickly when you are not moving, even on the warmest of days. At first I am careful to attempt to keep my feet dry. Finally realizing the futility of this feat, I splash through the puddles on the trail, actually feeling a sense of liberation. My feet can't really get any wetter; the squishing sounds are already hitting every note on the saturation scale. The trail, very treacherous with soddenness, finally sent me down on my butt - my first fall. It hurt - mostly my self-assurance. Sitting there in the rain, a bit scared, I softly cried a few tears. While struggling to stand back up with the 40 pounds on my back and gravity counteracting my grueling efforts, a fellow hiker came by and nonchalantly commented, "Wet day, huh? I have already fallen three times!" Three times - well! Confidence restored at the cost of another's misfortune, I happily continued on down the trail with a bounce and lilting squeak to my wet boots.

On day 11, I got off the AT for a one-mile road walk to a commercial campground called Rainbow Springs so I could get a hot shower. Singing ten days' layers of dirt and sweat off my body in this blissful first hot shower, I heard the voice of "Cooker-Hiker" from the bathhouse door, saying, "'Scarf', is that you? We have a car and a bunch of us are going into town to an all-you-can-eat buffet. Wanna go?" "Is a green bean green? Yeah! Town food!!" I happily replied from the quickly clogging shower.

Minutes later, giving the shower drain time to swallow my first few layers of dirt and not wanting to risk missing a ride to town food (food always wins in a confrontation of priorities on the trail), I crowd in the car with "Harrier," "Cooker-Hiker," "Freedom" and "Carefree," to head to the all-you-can-eat buffet. My stomach is growling noisily with the thought of my first "real food" (I realize that is debatable) since I began my hike. At the restaurant, I shamefully and gluttonously ate so much of everything, I had to then embarrassingly run into the bathroom and vomit it all up. Darn - all those green beans wasted!

Day 15 held a miracle. Actually "miracles" happen every day on the trail. Sunrise is a miracle; the kindness of strangers is a miracle. Water coming out of the earth is a miracle. Thich Nhat Hahn says: "People usually consider walking on water or in thin air a miracle. But I think the real miracle is not to walk on water or in thin air, but to walk on earth." I certainly felt to be able to walk this trail is a miracle. But some miracles are more remarkable than others.

This day I woke up with a really bad headache and stomach ache - the first time I had felt really sick since starting the trail. I could not hold any food down so I was weak. Being ill on the trail when you are hiking alone is very scary. I knew I just couldn't hike that morning especially since the first eight miles were straight up, ascending over 3300 feet of elevation! I hung around for a bit at the Nantahala Outdoor Center, where I had bunked for the night, but nothing was easing up. Well I also couldn't just stop hiking cause I didn't feel like it either. So I packed up and slowly plodded and drug myself up the mountain.

The only food that sounded good to me was dry whole wheat bread - yeah right. Whole grain bread is not quite a staple of backpackers being that it is heavy and certainly doesn't travel well, changing shape in a backpack to something totally unrecognizable from

"Wildcat"

bread. I stopped to rest at Sassafras Gap Shelter; while laying there wondering how I could muster up the energy to go on, "Wildcat" showed up for his lunch break at the shelter as well. I didn't relate to him that I was ailing; life on the trail is strenuous enough to everyone out here without having the drag of a whiner in our midst (besides we don't usually carry cheese on the trail either, which goes so well with wine). Settling beside me, pack off, pulling out his lunch he says, "Hey, "Scarf" you want some whole wheat bread? My wife sent me some in my last mail drop box and the weight is killing me so I'd like to get rid of it." Manna straight from heaven - bread.

My first complete zero day was day 20 in Gatlinburg, Tennessee. My friend, Leslee Barna, picked me up at Newfound Gap, where the AT crosses the road. It was so good to see a familiar friend's face! Wow do I deserve a day off; I have walked over 200 miles! For 24 blissful hours I was showered, wined and dined - how I appreciated these luxuries and good friends so much, except for when Leslee said, "You wanna go on a hike?"

Zero days, to explain, are low mileage or non-hiking rest days. They are called either zero days - if you hike zero miles that day or nearo days - if you hiked just a few miles. Zero/nearo days are odd and misleading, though. Since they are usually taken in a town, they are everything but a day of rest. Showers, laundry, eating out, post office, outfitters, phone calls home, eating out (again), re-supply shopping, library or internet café, eating out (again), showers (again), writing letters, packaging and mailing stuff home and eating out (again) - "Geez how many miles did I walk in this town today?" I wonder grudgingly for they are miles that don't count.

One of my favorite, though, and truly restful zero days, was a spontaneous decision to take a day off at Overmountain Shelter. It was just too beautiful there to move on. The huge old grayed log barn, the loft serving as the AT shelter's sleeping platform, opened out to a lovely view of a sloping meadow graced with sentinels of giant sycamores. Edging the meadow was an evergreen spruce forest right out of a Tolkien book.

Since it was not even near a town, it was a forced escape from activity. I actually, after first breakfast, even crawled back into my sleeping bag and dozed off for another few hours - what luxury - before having second breakfast. Later, writing in my journal, I realized this was Day 40 - how perfect! Forty days in the wilderness and then I rest.

At this revelation, I decided to go into the forest a bit and just sit on a log and meditate for a few hours, thanking God for this experience, for my safety, for His beautiful creation I was witnessing every day, for friends and the kindness of strangers, for support of my family and friends at home, for water, for food, for pillows... thank you, God. How we take so much for granted in our lives. Hiking the trail certainly enlightened my heart to many of the things I am grateful for that I had not given a second notice to before - simple things like a pillow. I remember a phone conversation I had with my brother, Wayne, from a trail town expressing to him how wonderful my night in town had been 'cause I had had a pillow to lay my head on. He later told me how much that comment had touched him and that night he, too, thanked God for his pillow. The simplicity of the trail makes the slightest gift feel like Christmas morning at grandma's. Day 40 was a truly wonder-ful day of rest, rejuvenation and gratefulness.

It was on day 24 that I could talk while climbing up hill. In the middle of an ascent, the realization that the conversation with a fellow hiker had not lulled into a gasping and panting discourse, sent me soaring up the mountain. This is a glorious telltale sign that I am getting stronger. Despite my general

Reunion with my Daughter on Easter Weekend

good health and all the prior-to-hike conditioning I did, hiking big miles day in and day out is hard on any body. But today proved long distance hiking is building up solid muscles and robust lungs.

Today I indulge, though, the well-being of my heart. I see my daughter, the first family I have seen for 43 days. How I have missed them! I am so excited but first there is Little Hump Mountain, then Big Hump Mountain. Zooming down that last slope to the prearranged road meeting spot, I spot her. Well it was a pure Hollywood, though genuine, reunion as we ran into each other's arms crying and laughing and hugging. Her boyfriend, (now husband) Dustin, who I had only met once, stood at the side watching, but was soon brought into the circle of hugs, too.

They took me into town and after settling in and

showering at a motel, we went out to eat - well they ate, I gorged. Chenoa was amazed at how much I could eat! We had two beautiful days together, took some short walks, snuggled lots, colored Easter eggs (a funny aside here - seeing a container of vinegar on the bathroom sink, not knowing that she had brought Easter egg coloring fixings to surprise me, I thought Dustin was a strange sort - what bizarre hygiene ritual would he use vinegar for?). Walking into the woods that parting morning, tearfully waving goodbye to my daughter, who in "real life" I saw every day, now not knowing when I would see her next, was one of the hardest moments I had on the trail to date. I just wanted to turn around and go back to Chenoa and home. That it was a rainy day sure didn't help either, though it fit the mood. The memories of those two days together helped keep me feeling blessed inside and I was relieved that the "vinegar mystery" was solved and I didn't need to worry about my daughter's choice of mate.

There were other infinite initiations for me on the AT. A tiny Bluet, the first spring flower I saw, had me jumping, well in tiny gay bounces at least, for delight - ahhhhh... the hope of Spring, the end of cold, the leafing of green. The opening day for being warm enough to wear shorts was cause for celebration; my legs dressed in white for the occasion! A sad sharing with other hikers was the disappointing news that the first hiker in the grouping that left Springer Mountain that leap day, had made the sorrowful decision to leave the trail and her fiancé. I had met them at the very beginning at Amicalola Falls State Park where AT hikers can register and weigh our backpacks.

Weighing my Pack at Amicalola Falls State Park

If you actually want to know this dreadful information - mine weighed 41 pounds. With experience, I later got it down to an average when fully loaded of 37. She and her fiancé, surrounded by supportive and excited family, were also weighing in on the outside porch there. They were all fired up, sharing with me and my family their plans to hike the entire AT with the finale being their marriage ceremony on top of Mt. Katahdin. Neither happened for this couple; long distance hiking can be extremely taxing on a relationship. We missed her and it broke my heart, reading in a trail register a few weeks later, an entry by her now solo hiking ex- fiancé (who continued on), "My backpack is too heavy, but my heart is even heavier..." Initiating first rites, celebrations or ordeals on the trail have different meanings and significance for every hiker, meshing into their own personal experience, one distinct footstep at a time. But I came to understand how our collective and shared journeys on the AT united our individual steps into a harmonious exodus as we all migrated south to north together.

The Zipper Symphony

"Satori," "Wildcat," "Moonpie," "Scarf" and "Harrier"

My fellow hikers absolutely swell my heart and soul. I expected a camaraderie to develop but not the deep bond that is formed between thru-hikers. I have never felt so a part of a group of people; normally I am a one-on-one person, more comfortable being with just one friend at a time. But this group drew me in with their unconditional acceptance of another hiker as just that - a fellow hiker on a very special journey - no other labels need attach. I belonged here. Everyone belonged here - what an incredible feeling! Along with this open-mindedness, the culture of long-distance hikers also demonstrates a depth of generosity of human spirit that you seldom see in the "real world." We accept each other without judgment. We take care of one another without hesitation.

I took a fall one evening on the trail and when I got to the shelter late, my knee gaping open and bleeding, folks jumped up offering help and bandage. Not so remarkable you may think. Well it is when you understand how very tired these hikers are at a day's end; we do not move once evening chores are done. It is when you realize these people have carried these bandages on their backs for hundreds of miles, painstakingly keeping them dry and clean. It is incredible when you appreciate that they shared with me - for they brought only one.

Every morning in the shelter, usually for me a welcome sight for it brought an end to my tossing and turning all night (I never did learn to sleep well in the shelters- more on that later in the "challenges" chapter), the sound of a solo zipper would give the orchestra its cue. Soon another and another would join the ensemble. "Daybreak, rise and shine," trolled the brass, "Time to start your morning chores and get on the trail again," hummed the nylon. I began calling this the "zipper symphony" and a more insistent alarm clock is not to be found. Peer pressure, even given unconsciously, is a prod in the rear. It is undeniably time to get up, no matter how sleepy or tired you still are or how cold outside of your sleeping bag may feel. Actually it is rather comforting and homey to hear the noises of your fellow hikers in the morning, as they roll up their bed, prepare breakfast and softly talk about what the day's hike holds. It feels so ordinary, like brothers and sisters in a family home beginning the day.

The evenings are reminiscent of a family home as well, as we each share our day's experiences, wonder about the next day and prepare our food together. At Piazza Rock Lean-to, in Maine, one hiker read to us a bedtime story from a book of Pooh he was carrying with him. "Wolfhead" delighted and impressed us with an incredible recitation of "Sam McGee"- a poem by Robert Service - a long poem! Evenings in the shelters were special as we each brought to the "family" our own uniqueness and gifts.

For what a diverse group we are! We have many different backgrounds, lifestyles, ages, religions and socio-economic statuses and yet we are all equal. Women are a minority on the AT but we are not catered to nor are we harassed. Seemingly the AT culture is untouched by society's issues and norms. No one imposes such standards, conditions or limits to life on the trail. Weaknesses and strengths are inter-mingled and shift. The stronger help the weaker and tomorrow's stamina may be rationed differently.

I had an excruciating day of knee pain on a New Hampshire grueling descent and when we got to the campsite the water source was more downhill. Anyone who has experienced knee aches knows that it is the

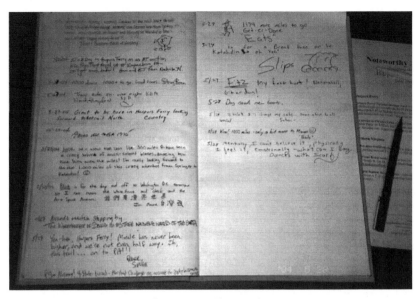

Shelter Trail Registers

downs that kill. We are mainly very independent on the trail and each take care of their own chores, unless a hiker is debilitated in some way. "Nails" knew I had almost reached my threshold for pain tolerance that day and she offered to get my water for me. When you are both weak, the one that can muster up a bit more strength does. It is an amazing and beautiful blend of independence and dependence.

Our system of communication on the trail is remarkable in its simplicity. Besides word of mouth, there is a network of trail registers in each shelter for hikers to sign in. Information, feelings, humor, poetry – whatever – is acceptable. Since there are north and south bound hikers important news of the trail ahead is passed on through these entries. We learn which water sources are good and that the next shelter has a leaky roof. Lost and found items are recorded, the best stores or hostels that await us in trail towns recommended and warning of acrobatic and delinquent raccoons at Gravel Springs Hut noted.

In this instance, the information was conveyed, but not heeded, at our loss. For the trail register alert proved to be true and was confirmed for us at this shelter in May. In the dark night, masked bandits climbed a smooth metal pole and broke into "Nails'" white food bag (hers was nearest to the pole). Hearing the racket in the middle of the night, she crawled reluctantly, but bravely, out of her sleeping bag, put her boots on and went to chase the thief away and assess the damage to her food supplies and sack. Before she came back to the security of her covers, she valiantly soaped the pole to insure the safety of the rest of our food bags from the dire villain of Gravel Springs Hut. We learned to trust trail register myths after that night. To replace her stolen goods we all shared our food with our heroine for the next few days.

The trail registers also tell us who has left the trail or who has been injured; hopes and dreams are intimately shared. The trail registers are read as eagerly as the daily newspaper is on a Sunday morning with coffee. We have headliner news, comics, "Dear Abby" columns, poetry (one hiker named "Haiku" would leave his trademark - a beautiful short poem in every trail register), weather, classifieds, advertisements, opinions, sports and commentaries. I could read hikers' entries for months - knowing their handwriting, their aches, their dreams, their adventures, their souls - maybe never even meeting them but feeling like they were an old friend.

One night a group of us were resting around the

fire at a shelter and a new hiker arrived. Introductions were made for her as around the circle we each gave our trail name. One tall, lanky guy said, "I'm 'Poptart'" and the gal laughed saying, "I've been following your register entries for weeks but picturing you as some saucy bitch!" Well the registers do have their fallacies!

The tradition of trail names is a hoot. It would be lengthy to tell them all with each story behind them, but I will share a few of my favorite. "Nails," the wonderful woman I met on the trail and finished with, gave herself this name in regards to her goal of becoming "hard as nails" on this hike. It was funny, after the hike was done she and I were sitting in a restaurant with her daughter, still calling each other "Nails" and "Scarf." Her daughter said, "Are you two going to continue using those trail names now that you are off the trail?" Of course – those are our names.

Most of my fellow hikers I never even knew their "real" name. "Seeker" was a sweet young kid with a long blond ponytail who wanted to become a minister. "Bear Bag Hanger" sleeps in a hammock tent instead of shelters or ground tents, looking like a big food bag hanging from a tree, a tempting morsel for bear. "Wing" and "Feather" were a mother and daughter team - wow was I envious... Self-named "Lucky Dog" left a beloved and supportive brand new wife at home so he could pursue his dream of hiking the AT. "Mousetrap" carried traps in his pack and would set them every night, trying to do his part in ridding the shelters of these furry varmints.

Which brings to mind several mouse tales; humor

me as I relay them. The shelters are notorious for mice; hikers accidentally leave crumbs which are feasts for wee ones. I saw an AT t-shirt in a trail town outfitters store with the slogan, "I sleep with mice and men!" Well before I lay with mice and men, I have the last chore of the evening - to hang my food bag or back pack from the ceiling of the shelter, lassoed tree or metal pole, furnished for this purpose in some of the spiffier shelters to keep mice, raccoon or bear out of our subsistence. I was many times the evening's entertainment as I tried to rope a tree to hang my food bag from. Yeah, I throw like a girl.

But mice are even a greater entertainment. Though hopefully underfed and certainly unappreciated, mice are a source of amusement at night - much better than TV. I actually became accustomed to them running over my sleeping bag-cocooned body throughout the night or hearing them up in

Food Bags Hung from the Bears and Raccoons

the rafters. One night, though, I woke up the whole shelter screaming. Sleepy but concerned voices said, "What is it, "Scarf," bear?" I knew I was blacklisted when with a squeaky and guilty voice I said, "It was a mouse." Well - it was the very long, furless tail stroking my forehead, as this brave little fellow ran right across my face, that necessitated the shriek.

Sounds of mice scurrying across the floor and rafters were as commonplace night noises as owls, whipporwills and nighttime insects. One happenstance one evening though, left "Nails" a bit perplexed till we figured it out. Settled into our cozy sleeping bags, luxuriating in being horizontal, listening to the natural night sounds, she heard an unusual sequence of noises. Raising her head in wonderment, "What! A flying mouse?" Then she saw the silhouette of an owl flying up and away from the shelter with a mouse caught in its talons, with a decrescendo of, "Squeak, squeak, squeak........." rising mournfully up into the dark sky.

One night the featured shelter entertainment was "The Glowing Mice Show"! A weekend hiker had in his pack one of those neon green glow-in-the-dark sticks. His grand idea of a light show for our enjoyment that dark night commenced with him breaking open the stick and putting some dabs in the shelter corners along with a morsel of food bait. We all settled into our bags to wait for the performance to begin. I have to admit I did lay there wondering if that stuff was toxic - poor mouse. Not being shy entertainers, the act soon began to our applause of laughter as three groups of four tiny neon green spots scurried and danced all around the shelter rafters, walls, hanging packs and floor. As I watched the "light show," my eyes sparkled with amusement from underneath my scarf; I was not taking any chance with my forehead this time. I wonder how long that green stuff glows for anyway?

I had an interesting conversation with "Miss Janet" when I was staying at her hiker hostel in Erwin, Tennessee. She was sharing with me that she had pondered for years, as she hosted thousands of hikers in her home, what commonality or trait successful thru-hikers had that insured their triumph of the trail, given all their differences of ability and motivations. She had finally found her answer and related it to me. "All successful thru-hikers are easily entertained." Our delight at that night's performance of "The Glowing Mice Show" gave credence to her conclusion.

Mouse tales concluded, now back to trail names. "Rainbow Brite" wore wild and colorful leggings to hike in. "Satori" was a delightful young person on a spiritual quest hiking the trail. Every night in the shelter, we each would salivate with envy over his meals. His awesome mother/food drop box supplier dehydrated each of the family's delicious homemade evening meals and sent them to him in his drop boxes. Many names are derived from foods, like the aforementioned "PopTart." "Moonpie" ate lots of moonpies, the number one food on the trail because it rates most calories per pound - important! "Pez" was always handing out candy pez's. "Stops for Berries" and "M&M" need no explanation.

"Dead Man Walking" is an older gentleman whose doctor told him if he tried to hike the Appalachian

"Hippie Longstocking"

Trail at his age he would be like a dead man walking. He and his wife, "Love Bug," climbed Mt. Katahdin seven months later. "Burning Boots" asked me one evening after a rainy day if I wanted him to dry out my boots by the fire. I immediately and vehemently said, "No!" for his name gave him away. The last seven boots, and still counting coup on unsuspecting hikers, he had tried to dry he had singed putting them too close to the fire. "Hippie Longstocking" is a wild gal, hiking in a short, red bandana skirt. She is a hiking machine, passing me on climbs like they are a stroll in a park. "Mountain Man" is a professional Opera singer in real life; we never could get him to sing for us though. "Camel" drinks lots of water in the mornings and evenings so he wouldn't have to carry so much while hiking. A liter of water weighs about two pounds.

Other self-explanatory amusing names are "Slipz,"

"Eats," "Sundance," "Pigpen," "Almost There," "Tortoise," "Gentle Giant," "Square Peg," "Cooker-Hiker," "Stump-knocker," "Pokie Puppy," "Fast Enough" and "Dirty Blonde." "Double-Wide" tried to refuse his given name, but couldn't shake it. Trail names are not always complementary. "LWOP," not able to retire yet but wanting to hike the trail, took a "leave without pay" from his job and gave himself that acronym for his trail name. "Nuclear" and "Ox"

"Nuclear" and "Ox"

are two delightful older gentleman we met in Maine. Coming out to a road crossing in which we had planned on hitching into town to enjoy its amenities, a note taped with medical tape to a tree caught our eyes. Reading it "Nails" with sparkling eyes said, "'Scarf', we have a date tonight!" The note was an invite requesting our presence for dinner with these two guys that evening in town. What fun!

The people I met on the trail truly feel like family and I have made some lifelong friendships. When you share intense experiences with people, like hiking long distance, a tremendously tight bond is formed. Some of these folks I may never even see again, but hold them in my heart for always. Some, I do keep in active touch with and we share time together, hiking more (yep, more) or doing other fun things. Though I had anticipated a hiking community on the AT, it exceeded my wildest expectations in its depth and level of enjoyment!

I could never express in mere words what meeting and hiking with "Nails" brought to my AT journey and my life. Throughout my childhood, every wish uttered when blowing out birthday candles, catching the light of a shooting star or nighttime prayers on bended knee by my bed, was that of asking for a sister (nothing against my three wonderful, loving brothers, well except for the times you.....), but a girl needs a sister. Adult wisdom has given me many "sisters" in differing degrees of closeness in my life whom I am immensely grateful for.

"Nails" is one of my favorite "sisters" and a treasure beyond words. Our spirits are kindred, our personalities attuned, hiking strides in step near perfectly -

the match was made in heaven I am completely sure of. How enriched my experience of hiking the Appalachian Trail was because of this amazing woman! We made pure and simple silly fun whenever we could to make the miles and packs lighter, like when we made snow angels on a bald in Tennessee or when we mooned the cog train on Mt. Washington. When one needed a lift, the other carried. It just seemed we were never both down on the same day, so we could encourage the other. The balance between us was just incredible! How blessed our meeting was!

"Sisters"

The Allure of Town

"Not all those who wander are lost."
J.R.R. Tolkien

No matter how much you love the woods, everything gets old after awhile. The trail passes through or near a town every week or so and the pull of civilization is felt in giddy anticipation days before the detour. A day in town is looked forward to as much as the sun's warmth after many days of rain. I think trail towns were one of my most pleasant surprises. I knew how important they would be for re-supplying, food, rest, showers and phone calls home, but I did not realize how much they would rejuvenate my heart. The town folks are incredible to AT hikers. They feed us, drive us where we need to go, give us reduced prices at hotels and restaurants, plus extra huge helpings of food and care. They let us sleep in their church Sunday School rooms, basements, firehouses, town pavilions, monasteries, barns, parks, even one - its town jail if there is an empty cell or two! It is hard to believe that people who do not even know us can be this kind and giving and most remarkable in this day and age - trusting. The true and simple goodness of people shone in these trail towns and left me feeling peacefully revived about the state of modern human-kind. Towns that shine above all the others are the ones that have hiking hostels in them; here we can bask in the camaraderie of kindred souls and shared aches in a restful state.

The first hostel I experienced was Blueberry Patch Hostel at Dicks Creek Gap in Georgia. The lovely proprietors, Gary (a '91 thru-hiker) and Lennie Poteat, posted in shelters north and south of their location scheduled times where they would be where the trail crossed the road to pick you up, taking you "home." Arriving there an early morning after just a few miles of hiking, I was indecisive whether to stay a night there or not because it was a gorgeous day for hiking and I hated to "waste" a good hiking day sitting around. But I decided my feet and knees

Gary and Lennie of the Blueberry Patch Hostel

deserved a break and Lennie's organic homegrown blueberry pancakes were reputed not to be missed. Yes, food is always on your mind.

To satisfy my heart, I call all my family. Though it is always wonderful to talk to them, it also breeds incredible homesickness that takes a gestation period before the re-connection births joy as well. I spread all my wet gear out in the sunshine to dry, shower, doctor my blisters, soak my sore feet in their creek, eat popcorn and pizza and savor the rest and sunshine, only feeling a little guilty for not hiking on such a beautiful day. There is a famous quote on the AT, "May all your zero days be rainy." It is not such a hardship to have rain in a town as opposed to on the trail. In town I'm assured of a dry bed that night in either a hostel or motel. I walk around in rain gear all day anyway while my other two "outfits" (one shirt and zip-off pants/shorts for hiking in and one shirt and leggings for sleeping in, two pairs of socks and undies and rain gear- that's all I carried clothes-wise) are laundering. Nothing can put a damper on the delight of eating at all the food establishments in town in one day!

Gary and Lennie at the Blueberry Patch Hostel were just awesome! Not only did she offer to do my laundry, she actually touched my dirty socks! When she brought me back my clean clothes, they were even folded. That simple touch of homey care meant so much and brought grateful tears to my eyes. That evening they invited all who wanted to, to attend church with them. My excuse of inappropriate and ragged, but now clean, apparel was met with Gary's reply of, "Oh they are used to me bringing along AT hikers and welcome you gladly." That they did. Gary was the song leader and changing the programmed song on the bulletin he instead led a song, with a smile towards us, having in the chorus a line,"... guide you on the rocky trail..." Breakfast made me cry from simple joy – a blue cloth tablecloth, fresh flowers, sunshine pouring through the window of the homey room, soft classical music and scrumptious home-made blueberry pancakes. Renewed in body and spirit, hikers were shuttled back to the trail to another blue sky and sunny day, extra excited because this day held our first state line crossing – leaving Georgia and going into North Carolina. I would certainly always hold though Georgia, Gary and Lennie, in my mind and heart.

After finishing the Smokies, a long time sought-after landmark accomplished, I was rewarded with Standing Bear Hostel awaiting me on the outskirts

Standing Bear Hostel, Tennessee

of the park. Run by Curtis, it is a rustic sort of place with a cute little wooden cabin built actually straddling a bubbling brook. That night I slept on a rough wood bed snuggled under several handmade quilts with the sound of water running under the floor boards beneath my bed. Pure and simple contentment! It was the best night of pure sleep I had on the whole trail!

Elmer's Hostel, actually called the Sunnybank Inn, in Hot Springs, N.C., is fabulous! It is a beautiful historic

Elmer's

Victorian house downtown and he serves organic and vegetarian meals. I shared a room with "Nails"; it had lace curtains, two lovely old wooden poster beds and a balcony off of it with white wicker rockers. We felt like royalty! We walked down the street to the Hot Spring Spa, which has been attracting bathers since the late 1700s. Single secluded little hot tubs are tucked in the trees along the French Broad River and we soaked our tired muscles in the healing mineral waters.

That night at Elmers held special significance. "Nails" and I had been hiking together off and on for a few weeks now checking each other out as potential hiking partners. Though I had wanted in the beginning to do this trail all alone, I had come to see how wonderful it was to have someone to share the experience with - joys were doubled, aches halved and dangers curtailed. We both had been feeling how alike we were in hiking style and in spirit; we were a perfect fit! So we discussed in that charming room committing to hiking the trail together, both saying yes! Dinner that night was ginger and broccoli soup, spinach salad, dill pasta with steamed veggies and carrot cake - yum! Elmer has the tradition of having a dinner question to stimulate the conversation. Our's that evening was, "If you could be a famous work of art, what would you be?"

"Miss Janet" is truly a piece of art and her hostel in Erwin, Tennessee, is a legend! We start looking forward to her hostel and her big heart for days and miles south. On March 31, after a bad night of "sleep," since eight of us crowded into Hogback Ridge Shelter, designed for six, we all were eagerly anticipating "Miss Janet's." We woke up the next morning to snow! What! I thought this stuff was over! But we all trudge in the snow toward town with high unquenchable spirits. Coming to Spivey Gap, where the trail crosses the road that leads to town and "Miss Janet's" haven, I shyly stick out my thumb.

I had never in my life hitchhiked before hiking

the trail where it is almost inevitable. At first I was very uncomfortable with this idea. But the choices are walk an extra 2-15 miles that re-supply day to get into town or starve - I don't think so. I got some very interesting and colorful rides. But I don't believe any topped this outrageous hitch! From Spivey Gap in Tennessee, the road is 12 miles down the mountain into the town of Erwin. It is always a bewildering feeling to first bop out of the woods onto a road crossing or, stranger yet, crossing over an interstate in a wire cage-walk high above the racing monsters below. Civilization comes roaring back into your life without even a prelude. Well except this time; it rolled into view- literally. We - "Nails," Rich ("Mr. Nails" joining us for a section) and myself, had been waiting at the roadside for a long time, with not one car whizzing by. It was starting to get dark (which makes getting a ride more dubious), we were getting cold with the night air hitting our sweat-drenched clothes and certainly we were (always) hungry. What were we going to do? Twelve miles of a road walk was too long especially in the dark.

Then, oh so very slowly, rolls up an old beat-up red pickup truck, gliding to a stop in front of us. A young teenager yells out the window, "Hey, I'd give you guys a ride into town but I am almost out of gas!" Well it is down hill to Erwin and food and gas, so in mutual and desperate agreement we all consent to endeavor a coast into town. We pile ourselves and our backpacks in the back of the truck amidst spare engine parts (I hope it is only gas this truck is missing), trash and an old tire or two, cheerful as can be. The adolescent kid (do you need a driver's license if you don't actually turn the car on to drive it, I wondered?) lets up off the brake and we start slowly cruising down the hill. Whenever there is a bit of a rise in the road, he starts the engine to get up it if our coasting speed won't push us up, then turns it back off, conserving the droplets of fuel left in the tank. Twenty gripping minutes later we roll into a gas station on the edge of town and Rich gives the kid $20 for gas. He innocently asks, "Can I put $19 in of gas and buy me a pop with the other dollar?" Do you think this was a scam?

Well the chronicle doesn't end here. This gas station being on the edge of town, no traffic seemingly around and not wanting to disturb the kid from his pop, we went inside and inquired if the cashier knew of anyone that could shuttle us to Rich's car, still a few dark miles away. She didn't, but offered if we hadn't gotten a ride by the time she got off work in an hour she would gladly take us. Thankfully, sure now our tribulation was soon to end, we settled on a bench eating some junk food from the store.

In just a few minutes a long black car pulled up out front. The lady smiled, gesturing. "There's your ride." We hurried out front to the vehicle to inquire if they would transport us, when the man got out and before we could ask said, "I hear you folks need a ride?" He was the cashier's husband and she had kindly called him to come get us, feeling sorry for us having to wait the hour for her to get off work. Thanks!

Well the conversation on our ride was very enlightening. We learned all about the local politics and heard about and experienced the town's ruinous road and bad bridge issues. When thanking the gentleman for the nice ride in his car, he alleged, "Oh don't thank me, thank the dog." Huh? Then he informed us it wasn't his car, it belonged to a dog. Come again? Well it seems, his aunt loved her little dog much more than she trusted her nephew and when she died last year to ensure he took good care of her dog, she had willed the car to the dog and the dog to her nephew. So the car was licensed in Rover's name. I don't know which is more unbelievable - a coasting truck for 12 miles or a car owned by a dog. This is a true story, I promise. Thank God we didn't need a third ride. Maybe we should have stayed in the woods; I think it was more civilized.

A big wooden AT with flowers planted at its base welcomes hikers to "Miss Janet's" front yard. Back-packs, boots, trekking poles, wet clothes and lounging bodies adorn her front porch. Inside is havoc with more bodies and gear than the house can swallow from gorging on hikers escaping the snowstorm. "Miss Janet" herself envelopes us with joyful care, not refusing anyone a dry and warm place. She energetically totes us around on the slick roads to stores, hospitals, groceries, trailheads for slack packs, restaurants, even some that have just had enough - home, bus stations or airports. After settling in at "Miss Janet's," not frightened away by a bit of white stuff (we've been in it for weeks), "Nails," "Mr. Nails," "Bear Bag" and I arrange a slack pack for the next day between Spivey and Sam Gaps - 13.3 miles. A slack pack is where you hike a section of trail in one day without carrying a fully loaded pack. There has to be road accessibility at each end to make them

"Scarf" and "Bear Bag"

feasible, of course. Hiking a bit less encumbered is a wonderful respite. Knowing a shower, town food and a bed awaits you at the end of the day is pure lushness.

So the next day, "Miss Janet" dropped us off at Spivey Gap. After hiking four and one-half miles the snow was so bad we couldn't see the trail or the blazes or even the footprints of the person right in front of us! At one point, Rich was lagging behind a bit (it is difficult to keep pace with seasoned thru-hikers) and "Nails" frightened a bit by the weather called for him to hurry up. He said, "What are my other choices?" She answered with a bitter, but sincere truth, "You walk faster or you die." "Mr. Nails" was soon panting at my heels, like a dog afraid of being left behind. Cold, scared and semi- lost we finally and grudgingly admitted defeat in this weather and were forced to do the forbidden; we turned back and backtracked four and one half painful miles that didn't count for nothing but smarts. Retracing our footsteps that were already obliterated by the heavy falling snow miffed, but we knew we were making a good decision; "Nails'" dire earlier words to Rich echoing in our thoughts!

At the road - freezing, anxious and annoyed - we finally got a ride back into town with a drunk man. Beer cans rolling all over the floorboard, the weaving driver constantly assured us he is not drunk and did we want a cold beer? Yeah, sure. At that time dying from an alcohol crazed ride was a lesser evil than from hypothermia in a snowstorm.

That night, at "Miss Janet's" with 32 days of hiking behind me, was the first time I really wanted to quit this hike and go home. I wasn't having fun and I tasted death that day. The next morning at breakfast "Miss Janet" read a beautiful poem about Mt. Katahdin, "Tacoma Ted" was playing a guitar, singing softly in the kitchen a lyric of "the people are the trail..." and somehow that notion left me. Of course it was April 1st, the fools day. Two days of rest, food, hot showers and fellowship, waiting out the worst of the storm and on April 3rd, "Nails" and I were joyfully making snow angels on a beautifully white carpeted bald, once again hiking between Spivey and Sam Gaps; forgotten were our previous footprints hidden underneath the angels wings made of white snow.

Damascus was a big milestone (459.8 milestones) for me. Not only does the trail go right through town, but it is well known for its annual event for AT hikers, "Trail Days" - three days in mid May of fellowship, gear vendors and repair, food and inspirational speakers. But for me it was also tangible proof that I was actually making progress north. Sometimes when you just walk, day after day, in the woods where there are no manmade landmarks like there are on roads, it is hard to tell how far you've come. It starts to feel surreal, like you are just on a big forest treadmill going around and around.

But Damascus was a concrete place for me. I knew how far it was to drive there from Springer Mountain, Georgia! I had driven that distance and now I had walked it! A feeling of accomplishment rushed over my tired but satisfied body as I stood under that welcome sign. I remembered reading before I began

Damascus!

this journey that by Damascus, 459.8 miles into the AT, only one-half of those "dreamers" that began the trail in Georgia will have made it this far. I felt fortunate; I felt strong! I got another similar rush of linear attainment, in Virginia, when popping out of the woods for a highway crossing and looking right I saw a green highway mileage sign pointing to Washington D.C. It really hit me then again the distance I have covered walking the AT. I have walked from Georgia to Washington, D.C. Wow!!!

We were too early for Damascus' Trail Days, being April 16, but it is still an awesome trail town with all the amenities hikers need and enjoy. After dumping our gear off at the local hiker hostel, we headed, yep you guessed it - to food! The Side Track Café had already been highly recommended to us as hiker-friendly and to my delighted surprise, who stood behind the counter but "Nuffy" (the Australian gal that had given me my trail name)! I had heard a few weeks and miles back that she had gotten off trail, so had assumed she was back down under. Instead she had decided to take advantage of her USA six month visa and look around a bit. She was working here temporarily to get a bit more traveling money for herself; her prior walking plan proving much cheaper than her new strategy of wheels.

Every evening the Side Track hosts a hiker sit down ethnic dinner free (donations appreciated) all- you-can-eat. That night was Indian fare - yum! There were fourteen of us around the family dining table that evening. "Mo," the only other woman besides "Nails" and me, started crying, saying over and over, "This is just so good, this is just so good..." We all shared in her sentiment.

"Nails" and I, with thanks to Rich ("Mr. Nails"), returned to Damascus one month and 383 miles later. He picked us up just south of Shenandoah National Park, which is where we had gotten to since Damascus in April and we drove back south for "Trail Days." How strange it was to whiz by in his car the exits for all the trail towns we had just walked by. "Trail Days" is a circus - vendors, tents, crafts, food and lots of dirty, happy hikers! The highlight for me was the Hiker Parade down Main Street. We line up by year you hiked the trail, "Nails" and I behind the last banner of "Dreamers" - hikers that haven't yet finished the trail. Spectators and town folks line the sidewalks on each side with yard hoses, squirt guns, water balloons, buckets of water and as we paraded by the fire station they even had a fire truck pulled to the curb with their fire hose aimed at us and on!

Fun at Damascus' Trail Days

Church of the Mountains Hostel – Delaware Water Gap

What hilarity! I always pondered if their objective was to cool us down or clean us up! That evening, I heard Warren Doyle, past AT hiker of seven times, speak of his AT experiences, with the moral of his talk being, "Flow, not maneuver the trail." The next morning I went to a church service, led by Bill Irwin, the blind thru-hiker. He said he fell on average twenty-five times a day. Wow - humbling. Then Rich took us back north to where we had left the trail and we just made it to the next shelter by dark. What a delightful detour!

At Delaware Water Gap, PA, I stayed at Church of the Mountains Presbyterian Hostel. I will never cease to be amazed at the generosity of trail towns, opening up even their churches for dirty, smelly, but weary travelers. That is pure Christian love. Towns allow hikers to stay in their local Fire Department Pavilion, city parks, a monastery's picnic shelter or the infamous jail in Palmerton, Pennsylvania. Churches or organizations in these towns sponsor hiker feasts. Some charge a minimal fee, but most are free or ask for donations. How these gestures warm my heart, rest my body and feed my bottomless tummy. Well, except for one.

On a lonely stretch of trail during an early November section hike, the lure of other people, a warm fire and the ever-optimist hope of food in the communal lodge of the Mohican Outdoor Center in New Jersey, turned me left onto a .25 mile side trail off the AT. I set up my tent and cooked my dinner, then hungry for companionship and always looking for more free food ("free" not necessarily meaning that of a monetary mode, but "free" in the sense that I didn't have to carry it) I headed to the lodge. It was a cool evening and they had a blazing fire in the hearth. Seeing no one but sensing a hospitable setting, I picked a book from the dark wood shelves lining one log wall and snuggled with a soft wool afghan on the couch, waiting for people and food to gratify my hungers.

Shortly a caretaker came over to greet me and informed me they were having an AMC (Appalachian Mountain Club) meeting there that evening, but that I was still welcome to stay there on the couch. Soon folks gathered around the long oak table behind me and commenced with their conference, completely ignoring me. That I understood. But when their business agenda was complete and refreshments of pizza and beer arrived, I was in pure torture from neglect. The one smell in this world that can make hunger gnaw in even a satiated stomach, let alone my near empty tummy, is the aroma of pizza! Of course, beer is the preferred liquid to wash it down with. They never offered me any of either, no matter how many times I cleared my salivating throat or paced around the fireplace to draw attention to my drooling face and sunken stomach or dropped purposely a book loudly on the wooden floor. Finally, disappointed to the tenth degree that neither of my hungers were satisfied, I moped back to my campsite, hoping I would at least get pizza, beer and good friends in my dreams that night.

Rob Bird, of the Birdcage Hostel in Dalton, Massachusetts, made up ten-fold for the inhospitality of the AMC meeting of minds and stomachs. After some difficult hiking days physically, mentally and spiritually, Rob offered all the comforts of "home." Showers, phone calls, grocery shopping, post office, etc. done, Rob then drove me to the next town's all-you-can-eat food bar. We had wonderful conversation in his living room with his dog, Tinker Bell, laying on the rug between us. How much homier can you get? The next day, being rainy, I decided to do a 9.3 mile slack pack, so Rob took me to Cheshire and I walked the AT back to his house in Dalton. He drove me to another diner that night where I attempted once again to fill up my relentless hunger. The next day brought a continuation of rain, so Rob shuttled me for another 14 mile slack pack over the beautiful Greylock Mountain. But finally, after three wonderful nights at Rob's, my slack pack options were over. With thankful but teary goodbyes and hugs to Rob and Tinker Bell, I was on my own again, with the renewed power of a visit of "home" to fuel me.

Monson is my last trail town; I have to admit I feel a bit sad. It is almost over, this journey of 2000+ miles! Shaw's Place has cute homey brightly painted rooms each even with a resident Teddy Bear. The all-you-can-eat breakfast of eggs, hash browns, bacon and pancakes is famous, but I don't see how I am going to walk after eating so much. After Monson, the AT enters the 100 mile wilderness - a remote section of trail. It is not as remote as it once was and with "Mr. Nails" joining us, we planned a slack pack the first 14 miles, returning that evening to Shaw's.

Almost immediately, we had our first "dangerous" river ford. A hiker, "Kokomo," had almost drowned here in 2005. Hearing his frightful tale the night before, where we surprisingly met him also staying at Shaw's (he was back on the trail to reminisce that horrifying experience), had left me with nightmares in which I fell in the crocodile infested stream and Rich had saved me, pulling me from the jaws of a big male. They had since strung a safety rope across the river which helped greatly and with Rich keeping the crocodiles at bay, the crossing was exciting, but not scary. Creek and river fords are daily endeavors on the AT. Some are just a happy splash across while others are boots off, pack straps loose and with trek-king poles bracing your footing you carefully inch across slimy rocks and rushing currents.

"Mr. Nails" has quite a challenge joining "Nails" and me, for we are seasoned hikers and he is straight off the city street. Maine is hard hiking and mid-day Rich was starting to drag and finally collapsed in exhaustion at Leeman Brook Lean-to. With three miles to go and rain and dark setting in, the situation became precarious. That is the big risk with slack packing. Since you are not carrying your full pack, if you don't make the planned miles, you can be stuck in the woods unprepared without tent, sleeping bag, cookware, etc. Coaxing each other along, this bedraggled threesome trudged in the dark and rain, slipping on rocks and roots every other step. It was quite horrible and scary. Finally coming out onto the road, hours late for our arranged ride, we thought to ourselves, "It is going to be very difficult to get a ride in the dark and rain." I wouldn't pick me up, let alone three of us, wet, smelly and darkness obscuring our honest faces. But we did get a ride from a very vocal Christian woman saying, "God led her heart to pick us up." She took us back to Shaw's where everyone had been really worried about us and had come several times to the road crossing calling into the woods for us. I felt really bad that we had troubled those good folks. They heated up leftovers from dinner for us and after a long and hot shower we were as good as new - well at least "Nails" and I were. Rich admitted defeat for now - what an admirable male ego he possesses to do such. He decided to let us go on without him and he would practice the art of trail magic and support instead. For the next week, pouring over detailed maps, he popped up in amazing places in the 100 mile "wilderness" with food, drink and generosity.

Four more hiking days left before Mt. Katahdin, we slowed the pace down to savor the last days - bittersweet emotions abound. Taking a bit of a detour we decided to take in Whitehouse Landing Wilderness

Camp- a fishing camp a mile off the trail on a side trail. Coming to the lake you blow an air horn and the owners Bill or Linda motor across and pick you up. "Nails" had read in the AT data book it had laundry facilities, so convinced me to go so we could clean up our clothes for the finale day. We got a big belly laugh at their laundry services- a lake, washtub and washboard. But they did have the best pizza I have ever eaten and Ben and Jerry's ice cream! It was a special deviation even without the laundry facilities we expected.

"Laundry Facilities" at Whitehouse Landing

Challenges of the Trail

"Life is either a daring adventure or nothing at all."
Helen Keller

   Before I even begin this testy section of seemingly much negativity, I want to liberate this gloom
by uplifting challenges to where they belong. I realize
it is a tired cliché to say trials are opportunities for
growth especially when one is utterly exhausted from
"growing pains." But challenges do seem to infuse a
greater concentration of gratitude for the subsequent
times of ease from pain or rain. Without contrasts
and trials on the trail and in life itself, we couldn't
experience abundantly their opposites of joy and
release. However tough this journey may have been
at times, and yes the trail brutally demanded from
me without mercy, an inner and outer strength, a
level of pain tolerance and a depth of body, mind and
soul perseverance that I just didn't think I had, I sum
it up as an incredibly wonderful experience.
   The difficult periods are simply ordained moments
to be gotten through. More so challenges met are
surprisingly and abruptly ancient history; just as a
mother forgets labor pains the instant the babe is put
in her arms, tomorrow's golden sunrise obliterates
the brutish previous dark day. Around the long bend
of a dry section of trail is the needed drink of cold
spring water or a welcoming shelter complete with a
gurgling brook. At the attained summit is a stupen-
dous view of ridge after mountain ridge stretching

into the fading horizon, making the arduous climb behind me, just that, behind me and the outlook before me heightened by more than elevation.

Actually the trials are not so much forgotten, for screaming muscles and knees and bursting lungs and heart won't let one slight the test, they were just simply over. They were done, concluded as part of a whole - necessary but not defining. Sometimes, I had the luxury of reveling in the satisfaction of achievement or completion. But most of the time even that would come later, at an accumulation of many climbs or days or miles. The individual challenges were simply met, one at a time. Then, with a gratitude magnified a hundred-fold because of them, would appear their opposite or a deep reprieve.

So I really believe contrasts are essential to enjoying life; they help to draw distinctions so that we can feel and experience fully the inverse. How could we appreciate smiles if we'd never shed tears? If we had no understanding of absolute weariness, how could we value deep rest? Could we ever feel the relief of being quenched, if we never feel the parchedness of utter thirst? I couldn't agree more with Helen Keller, for if not for these "daring adventures" life on or off the trail would be nothing at all.

Physical Challenges

"And the day came when the risk to remain tight in a bud was more painful than the risk it took to blossom."

Anais Nin

A great challenge in my daring adventure of hiking long miles was that sometimes I just completely and without respite for hours physically ached. In the beginning weeks how my feet hurt; how can something so small hurt so much? The more profound question is how did I learn to tolerate such pain. My back, knees and shoulders would scream sometimes, my lungs and heart would work past their fullest faculty, but it was my feet that could throb so horrendously at times I just could not bear the pain. Feet are required to carry the majority of the weight of walking 12-20 miles a day. With 35-40 pounds on your back, the chafe of wet socks and shoes rubs both new and old raw places. They really are quite small, I always pondered, to be obligated to take on the impact of the load of each step, each rock, the long miles accumulating in dreadful throbs.

Getting into camp at the day's end, I couldn't wait

Ahhhhhhhhh

to take off my socks and boots. If there was a cold creek nearby, away of course from our drinking water source, my feet would audibly sigh with thankfulness the second they touched the cool relief. This soaking and a horizontal no weight bearing night and they seem to always be ready to meet their responsibility again the next day. Of course, I had to promise them many things when I finished the trail - massages, pedicures, soakings, dry, clean socks and retirement of stiff hiking boots.

On extremely taxing days, utterly fatigued, I would think to myself as I trudged up another false summit on an empty tank - "This is a choice; no one is making me do this. Why am I here?" At the beginning, in Georgia, hikers were dropping off the trail like flies. It always made us kinda sad to hear that one of "us" was leaving the trail but it was always said a thru-hiker doesn't quit the trail; they just go "off trail" for a bit.

It makes me feel oh so much better that even the young kids on the trail hurt - feet, back, knees, shoulders, heart - they are not spared pain because of their youth. Why that makes me feel better I don't know. Though middle-age hikers are on the rise on the trail, it is still a fellowship of mostly youth. Before the hike, I fretted over my acceptance at being the "old lady" on the AT, at forty-seven years old. But then on the trail no one even noticed; not one person asked me my age the whole 2000+ miles. It isn't important out there. But it is noticeable inside - I would watch enviously as the young guys boulder jumped the stream in seconds what I was slow-poking, carefully working my way across. At day's end in the shelter, after chores, I'd lay exhausted as the young built fires or talked quietly for hours. I did envy them their agility, stamina and naivety. But I still made it to the same shelter, over the same mountains and crossed the same rivers. It just took me longer and hurt a bit more.

On the northern half of the trail, foot pain was traded in for knee pain. I guess my feet finally calloused over to a toughness no rocks or weight could penetrate. Then the knees could be heard in the next county screaming on the steep down hills of the north. They take the impact of body and pack weight on their wobbly joints when descending steeply. I experienced some of the most brutal pain I have ever felt in my knees going down Avery Peak in Maine. My knees hurt so much, stepping pain-fully down rock ledge after rock ledge for two miles, descending almost 2000 feet. I just vociferously cried and cried, my awareness of "Nails'" disgust with my babyishness just making me cry only the harder. I didn't have any other choice. I needed the release of sobs to deal with the pain.

Trekking poles really do aid, especially on the descents. I named my sticks "Yin" and "Yang" for their support in keeping me balanced. In reading about long distance hiking before commencing on the trail, trekking poles are celebrated to transfer 30 percent of the jarring impact of each step from knees onto their thin titanium limbs. I am grateful for my Lekis!

Hiking while sick is close to impossible. It is difficult enough at home to go on with daily routines when you are feeling ill. But on the trail, with its inherent physical demands, hiking when unwell is grueling. I was very fortunate to be basically a very healthy gal, so except for a few isolated days of feeling poorly, I was only deeply sick once on the trail. Unluckily, it happened to be in Maine, the most difficult state in my opinion of the entire AT. I caught the flu and was sick with it for over a week, with only the simplest of medications. Even the tiny ups were demanding for me. I actually felt like I was walking in a fog, oblivious to my surroundings much of the time. Dazed with fever, eyes blurred in pain, body aching all over, nose and throat raw with stuffiness, I moved unconsciously over terrain that required one's utmost concentration.

One day during this bout, coming upon one of Maine's glorious ponds - East Carry Pond - we just stopped and laid in the sun on the sandy beach for over an hour and watched a group of loons fish and then preen on the beach beside us. The sound of loons calling has to be the most magical and mystical music on the planet. Soaking in the sunrays and the scene gave me energy to go on. That night arriving at Pierce Pond Lean-to, I had my heart set on staying there given its reputation of being one of the loveliest shelter locations on the trail. I laid out my bag, preparing to try to rest a bit before I mustered up the strength to explore the special site. I sickly muttered, "...If only I had some hot chicken noodle soup..." It was extremely windy and cool that afternoon and while I was busy with my task, "Route 66" and "Nails" were discussing an alternate plan for the evening. Worried about the wind, cold and me, they pushed me grudgingly to move on a bit more to Harrison's Pierce Pond Camp, where there were cabins to rent so we'd be out of the raging wind and a consequently cold night in the shelter.

"Nails" rented us the cutest little cabin replenished with woodstove, oil lamps and two wooden bedsteads loaded with covers. I crawled into that inviting sickbed, clothes and all, while "Nails" built a fire and explored the camp. We did not have reservations, not planning on staying there, so the owner, Steve, was not prepared to feed us an evening meal. "Stands by Me" and "Partner," also AT hikers we had been hiking off and on with for several days, had made prior reservations. They asked Steve if he could stretch their dinner rations to have enough for me, since I was sick and in need of a nourishing hot meal - such are the hearts of trail family. The flu in me turned toward a healing arch that evening when Steve brought out three steaming bowls of hot home-made chicken noodle soup he'd had cooking all day on the woodstove. Moved and grateful beyond words, I slowly slurped the hot soup, relishing the miracle served me that evening. That night in our cozy cabin, laying in that rustic warm bed with piles of covers over me but still shivering, the perfect and hopelessly wished for comfort food in my belly, I contently watched "Nails'" profile as she wrote in her journal to the soft glow of an oil lamp. Though I was so very sick, I have never felt more well.

Another physical challenge was that of always being dirty. It did help that so was everybody else. Trying to sleep when dirty and itchy, was the worst nuisance involved with hygienic needs. Town days always consisted of at least two showers; one was taken just to get clean and the second for pure joy and muscle relaxation. Never will I take showers and cleanliness for granted again.

Many, many times due to these physical challenges, I just wanted to go home. "Quitting" lurks in the dark recesses of my mind almost daily. It is hard out here; it really is. I remember one day in Virginia, after a stretch of wet days, soaked socks and boots, I had some incredible feet pain; no amount of Vitamin I (what we call Ibuprofen on the trail), moleskin or a change to clean and dry socks would alleviate it. I had to just keep walking and as I walked all day I softly cried so "Nails" wouldn't hear me. My feet hurt; my feet hurt really badly. Despite attempted softness of my tears, late that afternoon "Nails" said, "'Scarf,' are you crying?" "Yes," I shamefully answered. "Oh..." she helplessly replied. And we kept on walking.

Mental Challenges

"Dwelling on the negative simply contributes to its power."
Shirley MacLaine

My research prior to hiking the AT often presented the concept that hiking long miles is more of a mental challenge than physical. Huh? But now I realize the validity of that premise. There were many, many times my body would absolutely not walk another inch and my mind had to transfigure legs out of gray matter and amble along herself. My brain talked, rather squabbled and bargained with my body quite a bit out there. "The shelter will be just over this

66

next rise. You will walk! You can have the Snickers when you walk just five more itty bitty miles. There, don't you see it? Down there. Can't you see the creek? A drink of good cold wet water is just a few more miles down this hill. You know water is always at the bottom, finding the path of least resistance you know." (which of course the AT does not understand nor practice) My mind could talk my body into doing things I never could get her to see eye to eye to! When even mental influence failed, you just didn't think at all and simply walked.

This usually happened when I came upon the dreaded MUD's and PUD's. What we hikers dub PUD's (pointless ups and downs) and MUD's (mindless ups and downs) can really wear on a body physically, but even more so mentally. They are especially irksome because there are no rewards of a staggering view on top or sparkling water on bottom. MUD's and PUD's exhaust the power of all three gears - body, mind and spirit. But if I wanted to stay away from succes-sions of ups and downs I guess I should have gone hiking in Kansas! Because the AT follows the Appala-chian Mountain Chain and chains by definition have a series of links and mountain "links" are not flat. Which brings to mind and body the "Blood, Sweat and Tears" song,"...What goes up must come down..." and isn't Appalachian a pretty word phonetically? It just kind of rolls off the tongue so pleasantly, which is not what I do on MUD's and PUD's. As you can tell, just writing about them makes my mind cease its function and I just ramble.

An exception to this aggravation and aversion to continual ups and downs for me was the roller coaster in Virginia. They are lying when they tell you Virginia is flat and easy, which is what I heard and foolishly believed in Georgia, North Carolina and Tennessee. The roller coaster lives up to its name with ten ascents and descents in 13.5 miles over an annoying bunch of ridges and gaps. For some reason, probably the austere power of attitude, I had a blast. I have always loved roller coasters though! There is even a warning sign at each end of this section of trail to beware! Yeah, I am tall enough! Part of the enjoyment for me may have had something to do with some awesome trail magic we had in the middle of the ride. "Cooker-Hiker," having read on my website that I would be doing the coaster section that day and living not too far away, had hiked in and brought us food!! Luscious, wet, juicy and cold food - strawberries and nectarines - every hiker's daydream - and lemonade and cookies. Refreshments

Sign at Beginning of the "Roller Coaster"

on a roller coaster traverse are quite unusual. At the end, I asked some fellow hikers excitedly, "Wanna get in line again for a second ride?" "No!" they all crossly huffed and puffed. I guess they didn't get strawberries on their ride.

Particularly mentally exhausting are false summits where thinking you have finally arrived to the top only then to find out there is still more climbing to do. Aggravated beyond reason, you just want to collapse and sometimes do, like I did on Little Bigelow Mountain (what kind of name is that anyway?) when I just couldn't take the teasing anymore. I would still be sitting there today but the mental thought and lure of the 2000 mile landmark just on the far side of her pesky flank drew me onward despite her mockery.

Weather

"This rain weeping and sun burning twine together to make us grow."

Rumi

If I have to name one reigning supreme challenge it would be extreme weather, with the five highest-priced and foulest jewels in her crown being those of cold, rain, heat, wind and lightning. Very many hours of dealing with any of those tainted trinkets and I would threaten to give over the kingdom of the AT to a stronger queen than I. They bullied me incessantly to hand in my hiking boots and made me lose all reasons for pursuing this vision. They could be, and were, pure hell at times.

I hate, I mean loathe, being cold. I always have. So this was a colossal challenge for me on the trail. To

Brrr... Winter on the Trail

make the date deadline at Mt Katahdin of October 15 (the park closes the summit to hikers after that date most years), I had to start the trail in the late winter to have the days to finish it. So many nights still got down to the low 20's, even a few in the teens; some days never reached 30 degrees. Some mornings my fingers were so frozen I couldn't open or close my zip lock food bags; I couldn't tie my shoes or wipe my butt. It is so hard to make yourself crawl out of a semi-warm sleeping bag, put on cold or worse, wet, or even worse, frozen and wet clothes, socks and boots. I would sleep with my water bottles so they would not be frozen solid in the morning. What are my choices? Quit or keep walking to spring.

The beautiful warmer weather with the coming of spring though brought her significant other - rain. There are no words to relay the groans of hiking day after day in rain. Positive attitude goes out the window without an umbrella. Weather report for today - rainy, 40 degrees and windy. On a day like that all you can do is hike; just cope in misery and don't think. If you think, you will think, "Why am I out here? I'd rather be...." This sort of thinking is a waste of time and energy, but it is hard to ward off.

Once after five straight days of spring rains, I was ready to quit. One or even two days you can get through, but multiple days with no break dampen the spirit irretrievably and launch the blister saga. Hiking for days with wet socks and boots would start my feet on a decline steeper than any mountain they were asked to endure. After days of being wet they looked and felt like homemade mincemeat pie. Furthermore there just isn't really anything one can do. I only carry two pairs of socks; boots take awhile to dry out especially if you are continuing to wear them through puddles. Sections of trail would develop into a creek bed that I just had to splash along. Trail maintainers do an awesome job ditching and installing waterbars on the trail, but even so there comes a surplus point to the best of rims.

Rain is hard. I would make a persuasive effort to focus my senses on the freshly washed scent of the forest, the lively pitter-patter drumming on leaves and the mystical veil of fog beaconing me into the heady haze ahead to hopefully distract my mind from drenched, wrinkled and tender skin. The shelter after a day of rain looked like the grandest Hilton and inside, out of the downpour, boots and socks off, I quickly felt like a queen again and could laugh, pointing a finger (one guess which one) at the rain demon outside saying, "You can't get me now - Ha!"

But if one doesn't watch out, it can still get you and cause even death - of hypothermia, a potentially fatal condition caused by insufficient heat, thus a drop in body temperature that can cause vital organs to shut down. I had one attack of this deadly state to make me take more care before I point and chortle again. Early in the hike in Georgia, I had a day of rain with temperatures barely above the rain/snow dividing line. Getting to the shelter, I made the mistake of attending to camp chores - laying out my bed, making dinner, etc. -before I changed out of my wet clothes.

I have my life to thank, for as my more-intelligent-than-me fellow hikers that night noticed me exhibiting the "umbles" - sure signs of an onset of hypothermia. Shivering uncontrollably, stumbling, fumbling and bumbling around the creek side with my full water bottles, my saviors inquired, "What are you doing, 'Scarf'?" "I'm getting water. What does it look like I am doing?" I grumbled and mumbled. "Your water bottles are full. Come on back into the shelter out of the rain and get warm," they advised with worry in their tone. I don't remember much after that for a bit, but they told me later they had to bodily take a cranky me back to the shelter, take my wet clothes off, put on my dry change. Still struggling and fighting with them, they then made me get into my sleeping bag. Force feeding me hot tea and soup from their own stores, I finally quit shaking and began becoming more sensible. Experiencing first-hand how fast hypothermia can set in, making its victim confused and disoriented, resulting then in delirium and bad judgment, really scared and humbled me. I have since read stories of rescue teams finding missing persons, victims of hypothermia, just feet away from their shelters, dry clothes, food and life.

Sometimes it would rain so hard and for so long the trail would turn into a river. The only way you could walk in this deluge was with your head lowered down, conquered by the pounding. In the White Mountains in New Hampshire we had a hard rain on a section of trail that was a boulder field. It was really strange, for the water made gurgling noises underneath the rocks that sounded like it was coming from inside the very center of the earth. It was odd. It slowed us down, so realizing we weren't going to make our planned camp we treated ourselves to an AMC hut - Madison Springs Hut, where after getting into our dry clothes, we sipped gratefully on hot tea and hot chocolate. Small comforts made huge by circumstances were appreciatively felt. It is sure tough to get out of a warm and dry sleeping bag, put on still wet and very cold clothes and head out into rain.

Its opposite, equal in testing for potential victims, is heat, which can literally drain the energy right out of the body together with the sweat. I could be feeling good, nourished, hydrated and after a few hours of hiking in high temperatures all is lost. Lethargy sets in and the competition of the sluggishness begins - the feet leading the spirit, no now the spirit leads, just a few paces ahead, then what is this, the feet again have taken the head, the spirit just lagging behind by inches...well you get the idea. I'd soak my scarf in every waterhole I'd come to for temporary relief, wrapping it around my forehead or neck. Conservation of drinking water was tricky; the heat and profuse sweating dehydrated you quickly. A breeze was a heaven-sent savior.

This brings up again the exquisiteness of contrasts on the trail and in life. For that same blissful, saving breeze in another time and place can be holy terror - wind. "Nails" and I were doing the long-awaited, but feared section of "The Whites" in New Hampshire. This mountain grouping was reputed to be our toughest hiking yet and weather conditions were notorious for changing quickly to ferociousness without warning. But the views and scenery are completely breathtaking. In fact, for me, without opposition, the trail

Franconia Ridge in New Hampshire's White Mountains

74

along Franconia Ridge in the Whites is the most spectacular scenery on the whole of the AT; it left me
awestruck! I feasted my eyes, walking slowly, savoring
every panorama completely. The alpine scene took
my breath away, filled my heart to overflowing and
soared my spirit like nothing I had ever experienced.
Since much of the hike here is above tree line, the
harsh exposure to the elements and rapidly changing
weather without warning can be frightening as we
found out a few days later.

On the gorgeous 5363 foot peak of Mt. Madison, we
experienced wind like I had never felt- raging wind,
blow you off a mountain kind of wind - 60 mile an
hour wind! In the south they would name this wind!
The wind was whipping around in every direction!
Crouching low on the rocks just below the summit
"Nails" and I discussed what we were going to do.
We couldn't even stand up! We certainly couldn't try
to walk with packs on that narrow ridge top! I got
out the map, barely able to hold on to it as it flapped
wildly in my white knuckled grip, to see if there was
an alternate trail to bypass the summit. We found if
we backtracked down the AT two miles there was
a base trail around Mt. Madison. So, though I am
usually very fussy and caring with my maps, folding
them neatly, having no choice in this wind, I just
crumpled up the map and stuffed it in my pocket.

So we walked back the way we had come, gradu-
ally getting below and out of the wind. Meeting some
hikers from France coming up, we warned them of
the conditions on top and they shared with us that
the trail around the base was even worse. So faced
with no easy choice, we trudged back up to face the

challenge. Once we popped our bodies over that top rock, it was each to their own wild and bracing ordeal. We couldn't hear anything but the whipping wind. It was brutish trying to stay upright. I would try to turn the pack away from the wind so it wouldn't be pushing me around then the wind would change directions. Once the wind blew me over down onto the jagged rocks and I bloodied up my knees and legs. The views were incredible when I could risk a glance around at them. I would stand still with both legs touching ground and wait for a tiny lull in the wind before I lifted one foot off the ground contact. It was the most ferocious wind I have ever experienced, let alone tried to walk in with a hump protruding from my back pushing me around as well. Never have I been so relieved to get back down into trees, grateful for their wonderful strong bodies and limbs shielding me from the wind.

Lightning is electric with risks, too. Hiking long distance and for many days, chances are good that you will walk in thunderstorms. Missing our ride to the Montibello Inn in Virginia, which would have provided refuge from a particular wild deluge, "Nails" and I crouched under her rain fly with blasting thunder and glaring lightning rampant in the woods all around us. We were afraid to set up our tents because of the aluminum poles, so with leg cramps and darkness settling in, we stayed underneath our pitiful "shelter." It was scary, but oddly and naively, kinda fun. I have always loved storms and go out in them usually instead of staying inside. But this squall made big noise and flashing lights, so it was a bit intimidating. Needing to move muscles and fear, one of us joked, "Too bad we don't have a deck of playing cards." That lightened the situation for awhile. Finally, the thunderstorm let up enough for us to brave the element of electricity and hurriedly we put up our tents, me rudely and blindly setting mine up too close to "Nails" so we were tripping over each other's guide lines. We only supposed the storm was the greater risk. Oops, sorry "Nails."

Snug in my bag in the Gentian Pond Shelter in New Hampshire, I watched the most incredible storm and lightning show from my sleeping bag looking down in the valley below. I was so thankful I was in the shelter and not walking in this light show. Another near miss from bolts of lightning was in the Saddle-back Range in Maine. The first peak was amidst lovely blue skies and scrumptious views, where I sat carefree in an alpine area having a snack. The next peak, The Horn, was terrifying as I raced a noisy storm that had moved in suddenly. The black and purple sky, thunderous crashing, forceful wind and flashing bolts of lightning close on my heels had me running for tree cover without a thought of the beautiful views around me. By the time I climbed the third peak, Saddle-back Junior, it was sunshiny again and I sat and enjoyed the 360 degree view, but forever grateful for the forest of trees below me, offering unconditionally their protection.

Fears

"Heroes take journeys, confront dragons and discover the treasures of their true selves."
Carol Pearson

Beyond this point there be dragons! Yes, there were a few dragons I had to fight hiking the AT. I had to learn to conquer several fears - getting lost, the dark, dangerous animals (bears, snakes, insects and bad men), technical rock climbs, falling and injuries. I have found in life that fears are usually much worse in our imaginations than they ever are in reality. But I do have healthy visionary skills and when hiking alone I had a lot of time on my hands and space in my imaginative brain to work up a healthy or unhealthy I should say, batch of fearful scenarios.

A silly, but nonetheless a very real concern for

Which Way is North?

78

Exquisite Winter on the Trail

The Greening of Spring

Gorgeous Hiking Day in Maine

AT Shelter in Autumn

White Blaze Amongst Red Foilage

The Dream Completed

me, was my worry of going in the wrong direction. In fact it was a good thing I had "Nails" with me on one section hike in New Hampshire because, dropped off by our kind ride from town at the trail road crossing, I put my pack on and turned south on the AT. "'Scarf'..." "Nails" said. Though the trail's general direction is northward, the twists and turns in the woods and mountains incorporate at some time or another every orientation on a 3-D map. It is surprisingly easy to get bewildered coming out of a shelter or after a break. Bill Irwin, the amazing blind thru-hiker, had a simple method to avoid this mistake himself. Immediately, when he arrived at the shelter for the night he would orient his sleeping bag with the feet end going in the direction he needed to go in the next morning. I was always careful, bordering on paranoia, to notice the direction I had arrived from when entering the shelter area or the side trail leading to it. With the utility of working eyes, I only left in the wrong direction once. When I came to that familiar log bridge and saw my own butt prints scooting over it across the snow I was mad at myself for hours. An extra mile! You may wonder how I recognized my own butt print; well I was getting pretty good at tracking in the woods and had added human butts to my repertoire of prints.

Speaking of butts and getting lost, another gone astray story - arriving alone at near dark to a shelter in Pennsylvania, I hurriedly used the daylight minutes left to get my evening chores done - filling up my water, fixing supper, laying out my bedroll on the wooded shelter floor, hanging my food bag and then lastly visiting the privy. By then it was almost completely dark. The outhouse is always a respectable distance away from the shelter, so noting the path signed to privy, I hastily took off.

Mission accomplished, I opened the crescent moon carved outhouse door and stepped down into pure darkness and headed in the direction in which I had come, I thought. When no shelter came into view I retraced my steps and took another bearing from the privy. Still no shelter; I was beginning to panic. "Stupid me," I muttered, "Why didn't I put on my headlamp?" After trying a half of a dozen different directions, I was really getting worried. I was completely, by then, disoriented. Roaming around, I finally even lost, too, the privy building! With no sliver of a moon on neither privy door nor darkened sky in sight to help me find my way, I was truly confused. Continuing to wander around aimlessly, since I certainly did not know which direction either the shelter or privy was by now, my blond head got completely ditsy, I mean dizzy. This is embarrassing. I'll just leave you wandering and wondering if I slept curled up on the forest floor that night or snug in my bag in the elusive shelter. Enjoy a blond joke or two at my expense as well!

Another fear born always at dark and greatly caused by fatigue-induced imagining is night noises. I have never been afraid of the dark; actually I love nighttime! But when I was alone in a shelter or camping by myself this fear sometimes seemed to creep in with the night stars. Nocturnal creatures moving around in the dark outside of an easily destructible sleeping bag and/or tent always strangely sound very big - very big, bad, ugly and hungry as well!

One particular evening in Shenandoah National Park, "Nails" and I were camping, she in her hammock, me in my tent a few yards away from her. We were both extremely tired from a day that had involved lots of climbs. Finally horizontal and a "what was that?" disrupted from one of our flimsy shelters. We had been bad girls and had not taken the time nor the non-existent energy to hang our food bags, instead using them foolishly for bear bait in our tents. "There it is again! It was really near us this time," we fearfully whispered. It was close and it was big! Then to my terror it actually rubbed against the side of my tent by my feet - "Yum, toes," it growled. "'Nails'!" I frightfully yelled, "It is right by my tent!" I kicked at it through my fatefully thin tent walls. I heard it move away, "'Scarf'!" yelled "Nails" as she kicked at the side of her hammock, "It is over here now." Oops- sorry dear sister of mine.

For thirty minutes or so this went on. The huge creature or creatures would not go away. Finally, I had had enough of missed sleep. Swallowing some bravery, I zipped open the tent and peered out with my headlamp in shaky hand into the menacing woods. I couldn't see anything but trees. "Good, I think they are gone, 'Nails'," I gratefully uttered. Settling back in the false security of our "shelters" and almost drifting off in desperately needed sleep, the dreaded monster returned. The scenario played again. "They're back!" one of us aggravatingly whispered. So on and so on the scene reran for its second season. This time "Nails" poked her daring head outside of her scanty protection with quivering light beams catching a pair of beautiful orange, usually brown, doe eyes. "'Scarf' - it's just deer!'' Relieved, but both feeling very foolish, we finally settled in for what was left of a night's sleep. I slept fitfully, though, waking up twice from horrible bear nightmares.

Being a good sport, laughingly the next morning, I shared with "Nails" one of my bear dreams. There was a mamma, poppa and baby bear (of course!). Fierce, though, in their red and yellow soldier uniforms they surrounded our tents with guns raised pointed at us! Weird! That day, though, we did come upon bona fide danger in the form of the biggest rattlesnake I have ever seen outside of a zoo!

Hiking happily, though groggily, along that morning, I commented on the buzzing noise we heard and inquired, "Are we supposed to come to a power-cut (they sometimes make a whizzing sound) this morning, 'Nails'?'' We both looked up overhead. Utility right-of-ways are great landmarks for hikers to get their bearings, since they are usually shown on our maps. If there had not been two hikers stopped ahead of us on the trail admiring the irritated, buzzing rattlesnake we would have stepped right on top of him seeing as our eyes were skyward! Coiled up to a foot tall, as big around as a man's arm, this brilliant black and yellow diamond patterned reptile was mad and rattling furiously at the two foolish young kids standing dangerously close to it. "Nails" and I made a wide berth around the snake, admiring its beauty and power from a distance. Walking on, eyes now focused downward, I thought, "Geez wonder what my dreams will be this evening?"

Some nights consisted of waking nightmares, for let us not forget, as if we could, the wee beasties. I have pondered a million times how something so small can be such a huge nuisance and what is their purpose on our planet. To be so little they are packed with power, able to metamorphose a lovely day or night into a miserable one. Except for a few weeks, I was able to avoid most of this persecution, since I hiked mainly off-season for bugs. So I was very fortunate by good timing from problems with irritating insects.

Though very cautious and wise in keeping myself out of risky situations with the human species, I was pleasantly relieved to encounter no problems with "bad men." At the beginning of the trail in the south, I was very heedful. Since I was at that time a woman hiking alone, at road crossings I would wait for another hiker or two to come and traverse the road in a group. In trail towns, I would try to hang with a crowd of hikers. "Wildcat" was an incredible gentleman on the trail, waiting for me at road crossings several times, if he knew I was close behind him. He stayed and camped in the woods with "Nails" and me once when we were just too tired to go the three more miles to the next shelter, though I'm sure he had the energy and would have preferred to go on himself. But extreme fatigue is a good set-up for silly stumbles.

Technical rock climbs are not my cup of tea or even my mug of something stronger; I don't enjoy them nor am I comfortable with them. I fear them greatly! Some sections in the northern half of the trail did involve some difficult rock climbing. The first that I would classify as a "semi-technical rock climb" was Lehigh Gap in Pennsylvania. Petrified climbing up that jumble of rocks, hanging on as I peered a few feet in front of me looking for reassuring white blazes that said, "Yes this is a trail," I was sure I'd fall to my death for what seemed like horrific hours. I was at last to where it leveled out and I sat there crying like a baby.

On top there were no soothing vistas or comforting forest arms, but a century old zinc smelting operation that had devastated the land. The Environmental Protection Agency shut down the furnaces in 1980 and the area was put on the Superfund clean-up list. It was horrible to walk through and with my frame of mind it felt and looked like purgatory. I remembered "Nails'" journal entry when she went through this area saying every school-aged child should be made to see this so they can prevent future destruction such as this. After suffering through this depressing annihilation, I slept fitfully that evening, chanting, "I hate Pennsylvania!" Sorry guys; I didn't mean it.

The lowest point on the entire trail, at 124 feet (the highest is Clingman's Dome, 6,643 feet in Tennessee) occurs at an unusual location— in front of the black bear cage where the trail passes through the Trailside Museum and Wildlife Center Zoo in New York. Of course, I disagree with this assessment for my lowest point on the entire trail was the afore-mentioned Lehigh Gap, lowest in spirit at least. I hated that climb and for me it proved to be my most terrifying section on the whole of the AT.

Second to Lehigh Gap was the 4000 foot Old

Speck in Maine. Again I was petrified! It is a horrible, ridiculous and dangerously exposed climb with tiny crevices for hand and foot holds. At times even these tiny aids were nonexistent and I pulled myself and my pack up the granite rock cliff using the branches and trunks of scraggly scrub trees that had managed a root hold here and there on the side of the cliff. I couldn't believe I was putting my life into the arms of a shrub that was fighting for its own meager existence there on the side of hard rock. Finally at the top, I collapsed in a trembling heap, crying, praying and cursing the AT. Halfway down the other side, I realized that I hadn't even looked at the view from the top of Old Speck, hard-earned that it had been.

Falling and a possible subsequent injury, is a very real risk and even a constant fear on some sections of the trail for me. For example, in Maine, with her nerve-racking cliff climbs. My first fall though where injury resulted was in a pine forest in gentle Virginia. In that jungle lived a fierce dragon, known for its gaping mouth encircled with sharp teeth. That day we had scrambled up, over, around and through the sharp canines, cutting incisors, grinding molars and two-pointed bicuspids of this rocky creation called the Dragon's Tooth. Feeling smug, escaping unscathed from its horrible jaws, we were now strolling down easy street.

After that demanding rock scramble the path literally turned into a smooth, level and pine needle strewn lane, where I hence tripped over a pine-needle? I still can't really figure out how I did it, but down face first in a plunge I went. Whimpering, eyes cloudy with tears, I inquired of "Nails," "Did I tear my pants?" "No," she, amused at my question, replied. "But you sure tore up your knee pretty bad." Hey, I have two knees out here on the trail, but only one pair of hiking pants, so my first concern for the latter is understandable. I carry a scar to this day on that knee, for the cut probably needed stitches but only got a butterfly bandage. I proudly tell how I defeated a Dragon that day, but was then wounded by a mere pine needle.

My second fall in which I miraculously escaped bodily injury, even nearly my possible death, was on Peru Peak in Vermont. I had no business hiking on that mountain during that time of year. My ride from town to the trail in a pickup with snow skis in the back should have given me a heads up that my own feet were not properly attired. Stubborn and stupid though I am at times, I waved goodbye to the smarter being and dove into the woods, snow and ice. The higher I climbed, the deeper the snow and crustier the ice. Really, wow, imagine that? Being early spring, some of the winter snow had melted but then refroze on cold nights, making nice layers happy to slide around on each other for fun and at hikers' chagrin.

I had fallen numerous times that day and climbing over winter downed trees that the trail crew hadn't been in yet to clear that year had me rushing to beat darkness to the shelter. At one point I just lost the trail. It is difficult with snow on the ground to see a pathway and the blowdowns had detoured me off trail. A white blaze was not to be found, but panic was. I was in a very dangerous predicament - dark approaching, high elevation which would mean plummeting temperatures during the night and lost. Attempting to stay calm and smart, I searched for a white trail blaze. Any would do: just a nice 2 inch by 6 inch white rectangle and I would be saved. Slipping on the ice-encrusted snow, into weird stances I could never manage in my yoga practice and probing the snow with my trekking poles to hold on to the icy slope of the mountaintop, I ducked in and amongst the snow-laden pines examining each trunk for my rescuing white mark. Full alarm had arrived by now.

Then I went down, sliding on my butt on the raw, cold, jagged and hard-packed icy snow, arms thrashing wildly and noisily about trying to grab onto a tree or rock or anything that could stop this death flow of gravity from taking me. My pack weight pushed me even faster, my trekking poles wrapped around my wrists biting into my skin in a death grip of their own and a piercing scream let loose from the depths of my soul, as down, down I slid to a sure death. Then I hit perfect ominous silence. Did I reach bottom? Am I dead? I open my terrified eyes and found myself against a tree, stopped, but hanging at the very edge of a cliff. "Oh my God," I prayed as I looked up. Heaven-sent aid in the form of a white 2x6 inch rectangle on the tree that had stopped my plummet over the brink of the precipice met my terrified eyes. In that upward gaze, seeing that white blaze on the tree I was most humbled. Indebted for my life, I uttered my prayer of thanks- giving and in giddy relief and in the release of healing laughter, I giggled at the white blaze on my savior tree. Checking my body for injuries, I then slowly and carefully stood and followed the white blazes on to my shelter, arriving right at the verge of dark but with a light in my soul that could never be extinguished. For I had the Master Dragon Slayer on my side that incredible day.

But did I learn a lesson? Yes, I got off the trail at the next road crossing and skipped up several miles to continue my hike in lower elevations to give spring time to do her magic melt down dance. Then later I returned to hike the higher mountain peaks I had skipped. Smart move, "Scarf!"

Sleeping

"The universe – being alive, these are your lovers."
Living in the Light

"What a lousy night of 'sleep'!" I grudgingly uttered many mornings, especially directed toward the well-rested snorers who shook the wooden platform floor of the shelter all night. Even using ear plugs, fellow hiker snorers were a real problem for me being that I am an extremely light sleeper (must have been all those years of mother conditioning). There is nothing so tormenting to a weary body and mind as a loud snoring and snorting bedfellow. Tossing and turning all night trying desperately to fall into sorely needed sleep despite the racket, I would entertain myself, not counting sheep, but devising methods of silencing the offender short of murder. It was pure torture for me (and them – heeheehee).

If I was fortunate to have a quiet shelter, I still had difficulty staying asleep on the hard surface where my body lay. Cold, hot, bugs, itchy, dirty, hungry, bursting bladder, thirst, fear, anxiety, weird dreams, sore hips, quivering legs and feet, all twisted and turned as they vied equally to be noticed. My reader may wonder why I continued? I wonder, too. What was the balm to these trials of the night? The night sky and sounds, relief from at least verticalness and heaviness of pack and the gratification of the days achievement would somehow console these rest-less nights. It was rest of a sort. So after my initial aforementioned gripe I then willingly would greet the morning with, "Hey a new and exciting day! I wonder what will be around the next bend in the trail?" My amazing body and spirit were somehow able to capture enough rest in those tosses and turns to hike another day.

Autumn Leaves

"You are as powerful and strong as you allow yourself to be."

Robyn Davidson

Hiking in autumn was spectacular. The forest dressed in her fall splendor, framed in a blue dream of a sky with crisp air invigorating each intake of breath. You are simply so glad to be alive and in the woods. But I did not anticipate the hidden and unusual challenge of fall time - a bronze carpet of sneaky and slippery leaves. I slipped constantly when going either up or down on their slick texture, oak and elm leaves being the worst. My brother Wayne laughed at this impor-tant to me, but of trivial value to most, knowledge of which leaves made for the most slippery surface to

Autumn Trail

walk on. Also the covering of newly fallen leaves caused the trail to blend in with the surrounding forest floor, camouflaging it with many wrong ways. Again thank God and trail crews for white blazes.

Monotony

"The very least you can do in your life is to figure out what you hope for. And the most you can do is live inside that hope."

Barbara Kingsolver

I truly love the deciduous forests and mountains of the eastern United States. The plant diversity is amazing! Still, walking dawn to dusk, weeks on end, even this remarkable variety can begin to feel monotonous. Mornings I would hike happily along, singing with dawn a favorite Jim Stoltz song "Morning in the Mountains" - "...there's a glow in the east...the start of a brand new day... so live each day like you mean it, revel up each dawn that comes your way and if it's blessings you're a'counting try a morning in the mountains, there ain't no better way to start the day.....''; but by noon I was lamenting my own version to a Jim Croce song "...walking on the AT blues..." Such is life on the trail.

Hiking in winter in a void of color, sometimes absolutely as exquisite as a Christmas card scene, other times only felt black, gray and white, day in and day out simply drove me mad. I can remember the awe I felt when I saw the first glimpse of green grass on Roan Mountain. I have never appreciated simple turf so much before walking for weeks in winter woods with only white, brown and gray around me and beneath my feet. Though the snow is lovely as it carpets the forest floor and mountain angles, I was just ready for a remodel to green rugs. Sitting down in the emerald grass, boots and socks off, I enjoyed running my toes through the cool, silky blades, the nap brushing the weariness of the miles away. Do I have to move?

For lack of a better word, I will label the tiresome ups and downs monotonous. If there were views on top of the mountains, the climb always felt worth the effort; if none it was hard to not resent the climb as a lot of exertion for naught. False summits, those climbs where you are just sure this will be the top of the mountain, only to find at that crest another one rising before you with a smirk on its flank, are maddening as well. Why is it always that the last 200 feet of climbing is so much harder than the preceding 2000 feet? Hiking in a section in New

Hampshire, I was stewing into a boil of exasperation on a series of steep rock climbs up and down the Wildcats - Wildcat E, Wildcat D, Wildcat C, Wildcat B and Wildcat A. Come on!!!! Surely they could have come up with some different names so I didn't feel like I was on a repetitive arduous climbing nightmare escalator. I think you can thus understand why when "Nails" and I got to the road crossing the next day near Gorham, New Hampshire we opted to get off the trail and go to the Maine coast instead and eat boiled wildcat, I mean lobster.

At times, it wasn't any particular tedium, it was just I was completely burned out on walking the trail. All the challenges accumulated into huge discontent - being dirty all the time, physical fatigue and pain, the hunger for "home," dealing with adverse weather and lack of a good sleep. Reading back in my journal, several times I wrote entries such as these - "It seemed like all day was up hill! I am very, very tired. I hate the AT! I hate how I am driven to complete it! I am so very tired. Did I already say that? How hard this is! How tired I am! How sick in mind and body and spirit I am of this damn trail!"

Most the time, though, after a day feeling like this, some natural high would occur to turn my feelings around. One exhausting day of hiking in rain and snow with some difficult rock scrambles in New Hampshire, my whole body was in a very bad mood. Then a few miles from the shelter, walking through a glistening freshened pine forest, the rain stopped and all the birds in the forest started to sing. I have never in my life heard so many different types of birdsongs all at once. It was almost tropical. I love what Maya

Angelou said, "A bird doesn't sing because it has an answer, it sings because it has a song." Those birds joyfully singing kept my own heart in song and my feet in beat those last few miles into camp.

Once though, simply beat, I just got off the trail unplanned at the next road crossing and hitched to the nearest town. I didn't want to walk another foot. I got a motel room, bought an incredible amount of food, propped my feet up in the bed and watched TV all day – three movies and several worthless sitcoms. It was great to just not walk and not think! TV does that to you, you know. The only time I moved the whole day was a few times I'd get up and look out the window and grin at the rain. The next morning, I had planned to have another day of the same. After watching about an hour of TV, I thought yuk – enough! Miraculously healed, like an adolescent pleading a bellyache to get out of going to school only to have his mom suggest since he was home all day he could watch his baby sister, I set back off on the trail. It took only one day to burn me out on TV.

Hunger

"Abundance is in large part an attitude."
Sue Patton Thorle

While I do agree with Sue Thorle that abundance is an attitude, burning the calories I did hiking strenu-ously for hours, days and weeks on end, I just did not always have a wealth of energy no matter how much I put into my mouth or mind! I always felt hungry. I ate larger quantities of food in trail towns than even my three brothers together growing up could

Cooking in the Shelter

devour! Food fantasies are a constant entertainment as I walk. That is why "trail magic" in the form of food is so appreciated.

"Trail magic," by the general classification, is when the "universe" seems to give you just what you need at that time- for example when an unknown "trail angel" leaves some goodies (usually food and drink) along the trail for the hungry hikers as they pass by later to nibble on. The offer of extra food, food that we didn't even have to carry, was to continu-ally ravenous hikers definitely magic! The first time I experienced this type of trail magic I actually, later very regretful, passed it by thinking the old Styro-foam cooler was trash some horrible soul left in the woods. That evening in the shelter when everyone was expressing gratitude for the delicious orange juice, donuts and apples left in the white cooler that morning for us starving hikers, I was sick with emptiness - darn! Another creative giver of trail magic put granola bars in the trees for a good mile of trail. Hanging on a tree branch would be a bag of apples. We never take more than one, leaving some magic for the next hiker. Hiking on Easter Day, an Easter Bunny Angel had left chocolate eggs laying alongside the trail. There is controversy over leaving food and containers in the woods because of the risk of wild life eating unnatural food and the containers becoming litter. Trail angels are requested to come back and pick up what is left and many do. That strangers, though, would walk and pack food in and out of the woods to leave for hikers they didn't even know nourished much more than my body.

Once I came down off a mountain to a road crossing and there was a couple with a grill set up cooking hamburgers and hot dogs. Offering me a plate with one of each hot off the grill they pointed to a cooler of assorted condiments, cold drinks, fruit and homemade brownies. They were feeding hikers as we came out of the woods. "Why?" I asked them. Their son was hiking the trail that year and this was their way of thanking the strangers that were being kind and giving to him. In Maine, a woman named Lisa was walking in the early morning up a section of trail near her home, handing out her homemade zucchini bread; it was still warm - oh tastes of home...

But trail magic for me was also a beautiful blue sky after days of rain or birds singing at days end to serenade you those last difficult miles to the shelter. The simple kindness of strangers in a trail town or a fellow hiker pulling your weight when you can't carry it is special magic, too. There are endless examples of cherished blessings on the trail to comfort me as I met the many challenges that each day brought. But food certainly ranks very high to insatiable hikers.

Leaving the Trail

> "Four rules for vital living:
> Show up.
> Pay attention.
> Tell the truth.
> Don't get attached to the results."
> <u>Roads Home</u>

My decision to go "off trail" for awhile, after hiking continuous for eighty-eight days and 1008.6 miles covering five states, was one of the most difficult, but easy choices I have ever had to make. The love of a daughter significantly outweighs the power of a dream, though they are both potent. The pull of that mighty Mt. Katahdin was enormously strong but the simple tug of my child's hand was even mightier. My children are and always will be my truest dreams come true and my priceless priority.

My youngest, a daughter and my best friend, Chenoa Joia, had left home to go to college that fall '03 and secured a summer '04 job at a camp. She left a door of my life gaping wide open and the rooms within very empty. She wouldn't be home that winter, spring and summer and feeling a little loss of purpose, the "not yet" ocean wave began lapping outside that ajar door. What better way to relieve my "empty nest" melancholy then to pursue my AT dream. So out the open door I went to go frolicking in the waves of the Appalachian Mountains.

February '04 I had left to thru-hike the AT, which usually takes about six months. The summit deadline for Mt. Katadhin is October 15, so I had allowed an extra month or so to cushion my "older" body. My daughter's summer plans changed, though, when she broke her ankle playing frisbee in her fiancé's front yard; hey I thought I was the one taking all the risks! So she was going to be home that summer after all. To go on record here, Chenoa never, never put any pressure or guilt on me to get off the trail; quite the opposite she encouraged me not to get off for her, but continue my dream. But my heart would not even think of missing an opportunity to have more time with my adult child at our home. The AT will always be there; my daughter's era for living at home was drawing to a close. I will never forget, but cherish always, her words affirming that I had made a good decision. When I got home from the trail that early June day, greeted by my daughter's loving arms, my heart swelled to overflowing from her words, "Momma, I feel so very loved!" I had done the right thing.

Actually the most heart-wrenching and challenging part of this decision was not leaving the trail (I'll be back!), but parting from my new-found hiking partner and "sister"-"Nails." That was emotive torture of the deepest kind. She had made the decision to continue on with a nephew who was going to join her. At the junction of our two decisions, beside the quickly rising from our tears Potomac River at the Maryland State line, our sixth state, we cried like babies who are hungry, wet, teething, constipated and have a diaper pin piercing their hearts all at the same time. We kept looking back at each other-waving, crying, hearts breaking... What a forever bond we had forged there on the trail together. We are sisters/friends for life.

I was picked up at Harper's Ferry, West Virginia, where I got off the trail, for a special visit with my priceless friends, the Colemans, before I went home. I had met Dan Coleman almost twenty years earlier during his own incredible pilgrimage of biking across the United States from the Pacific Ocean to the Atlantic Ocean! I noticed him and his friend with loaded bike panniers at the park in my home in Kentucky. Always drawn to a fellow traveler like ants to a picnic, I went over and struck up a conversation that resulted in a lifetime correspondence with Dan and his family. I invited them to stay at my home/ land for the night and they were as delighted as I to share time together. They shared their adventure with me, played with my children, helped me can blackberry jam and willingly, though suspiciously, ate my tofu dinner.

After he completed his cross-country ride his mother, Lou Ann, wrote me a thank you note for showing her son hospitality. So another trusting turn began an instant connection and friendship between me and her and her husband, Robert, who was the Coleman that picked me up at Harper's Ferry and took me to their home. I had a wonderful reunion with Dan, his wife Pam and their delightful girls Ellery and Ruby. I was reminded afresh that in traveling it is the people you meet that touch the heart in such far-reaching and unsuspecting ways. A simple offer of food and shelter to a weary explorer in a strange land has in return given me the enrichment of this lovely family in my life. In honor of our reunion, for dinner that night Dan fixed tofu for me. Not being the typical hiker fare, but a staple of my life at home, it was delicious and memorable.

After this holiday at the Coleman homes, my always supportive, mom, brother and sister-in-heart picked me up back in Harpers Ferry. Mom and I embraced and cried; it was so good to see family. I saw members of my "trail family" as well, just arriving in town off the trail and it was bittersweet to see them and tell them I was leaving the trail. "Nails" was in town, too, taking some zero days to regroup, so my family and I met her, her husband Rich and her nephew for a celebratory dinner. I gave her a blank journal - a

Temporary Parting from "Nails"

book for us to write down the 100+ adventures she and I are pledging our lives on to get into! Oh how I am going to miss her.

Sitting in the backseat with my family as they drove me home, a multitude of mixed and raging emotions were going on inside of me. Fulfillment of what I had completed (walking over 1000 miles IS something to write home about!) jumbled with a sense of failure. My dream – I gave it up; I quit before it was completed. Pride of at least beginning it and completing almost half of it warred with a sickening shame of failure. Empty with full, gains among losses and regrets, fought with relief. I wondered and worried if my supportive family and friends were disappointed in me for not completing the trail this trip. Happiness of having my daughter home for the summer and time to let my body heal and restore energy at this potent and confusing ending point, barely won over the sadness of leaving my dream and "Nails." How can I feel such opposing emotions at the same time? I was quiet there in the backseat, too much inside of me trying to find a place to settle, going faster in that car than I had dreamed of going for three months, speeding farther and farther away from my identity of "Scarf." In the motel room that night, my mother nearly cried when she saw my feet, saying, "Honey, they look like ground turkey." They felt like ground turkey; how had I been walking on them every day?

To help those still walking and to give back to a trail and people that have given me so much, I involved my willing and giving family in a bit of trail magic. Driving back through Shenandoah National

Park on the way home to Kentucky, we hung some bags of goodies on the trees by the trail crossings. We even walked on a section of the AT that I had hiked just weeks before and found and read at a shelter my own journal entry - "5/22 Blue sky day appreciated. Ate too much at the wayside and got lazy. Peace, 'Dances With Scarf.'" Oh the call of the trail is pulling me back in and I keep my beloved daughters' face close to rein in my faltering heart. Later there will be time for the AT again; I will return. I am just going "off trail" for a bit. I will reach Mt. Katahdin. Now is time to reach lovingly for my precious child's hand.

A note here to put all my previous and subsequent stories in an assemblage of chronological order - "Nails" did continue hiking for another month, then got off the trail for family reasons as well. After sharing that lovely summer with my daughter, I resumed my hike as a section-hiker. Section-hiking is defined as one that hikes the trail over several years, as opposed to a thru-hiker who does it all in one year. So starting that same year in early November '04 after Chenoa went back to college, I was back on the trail until winter hit and I couldn't safely hike. So hiking sections every spring and fall, working around my seasonal park ranger job, I eventually caught up to where "Nails" had ended her hike. Then, in immense gratitude and joy we began hiking sections together and completed the trail together (summit day story later☺) in September 2007.

Section-Hiking

It takes much more faith, vision, courage and perseverance, I feel, to hike the AT as a section-hiker than as a thru-hiker. Becoming re-engulfed back into your "other life" between each section, it can be easy to give up and not return again and again to the trail. Arranging transportation to and fro the trail over and over takes dedication, planning and skill. Keeping or reconditioning your physical body to handle the hiking is not easy. Also as a section-hiker you do not usually become as part of a "trail family" as you do with thru-hiking, so you are alone more, especially hiking "off season" as I did.

So hiking as a section-hiker was a very different experience for me than my months as a thru-hiker. Gone was my "trail family", that group of people who, having about the same walking pace as we move north together, form a family unit of sorts. We get to know one another well - moods, strengths, weaknesses, humor, dreams - and look forward to reuniting in shelters or campsites at day's end for fellowship and sharing. It is easier, it seems, to disclose and slip secrets and share deep yearnings in the dark or around a campfire; it is as if the darkness protects the unveiling from predators judging our feelings. I missed those communal times, for as a section-hiker, if I did come upon thru-hikers, I was added to the mix when the soup had been simmering awhile and the flavors had already merged into a finished creation. I was like the bay leaf, added for a bit and then taken out, only leaving a slight new taste and not really ever a major part of the gumbo.

Sometimes I was hiking alone without seeing absolutely anyone for days, even weeks. Since I had returned to my seasonal Park Ranger job when getting off the trail that summer, I could only hike the AT before and after my work season – November and March/April. This put me on the trail off season for thru-hikers; early winter thru-hikers had completed or gotten off trail. Early spring they were all in Georgia, not north where I was picking up where I had finished in May. I also didn't even see day or weekend hikers; it just wasn't a favorable time of the year for most people to be out hiking. I was totally alone the majority of the time.

It is not really rational to compare section-hiking and thru-hiking. They are just different. I feel I appreciated the trail more as a section-hiker. I knew I was only out there for a two-to-six week period of time, so gifts became more precious and challenges more tolerable. Solitude developed my spirituality to a higher level than I thought possible and I will forever be grateful for that growth. Also there is a sense of empowerment and a growing self-esteem that doing alone brings that I didn't experience as much when hiking with someone. The flip side of that is the fear factor that rises more so when hiking alone and the loneliness in the omission of a community of hikers.

For I did really MISS a "trail family." People proved to be a big part of the trail experience. Reading the shelter journals at night was richer when I knew the folks who wrote the entries. I had shared a lunch and vista with them the day before or drank holy water together from the cold brook a ways back. I loved feeling part of a group; as I said earlier I have never had that experience in my life being a loner at best. I missed "Nails" so much in the sections I hiked without her. Somehow the AT and she and I had blended into one. So I was so very grateful that fate and circumstance enabled us to hike together again in New Hampshire and Maine. Finishing together was perfect! But first there was the mid-Atlantic states to catch up to where she got off.

Loneliness

"We can let our lives be directed by that same force that makes flowers grow or we can do it by ourselves."
Marianne Williamson

I remember my first day back on the trail that early November; I had forgotten the feeling at day's end when you anxiously watch for the shelter around every long bend. Have I missed it? Where is it? Who will be there already? My abode for my first night back on the trail was Rocky Run Shelter in Maryland. It was a great shelter with a cooking area away from the shelter and even a porch swing. But no one was home. The "kitchen" was empty of the scuttling of a family's meal preparation. There was no one to rock gently with me on the swing, resting our tired feet talking about the day or what the morrow would bring. It was strange to be there by myself; I missed the comradery. I missed my sister "Nails." I felt so utterly alone.

Walking the Trail Alone

That past summer, as a thru-hiker, when I was walking with the "pack" that leaves Springer Mountain every spring, I did not have one single night alone. Now I was totally alone most every day and night. I did my camp chores in the evening quietness. It is perplexing how quickly the hiking routine becomes familiar again when you've been off the trail for a few months. It truly feels like my home away from home - this Appalachian Trail does. Spreading out my lone bed roll on the roomy wooden floor, hanging my solo food bag, which made slim pickings for a hungry bear, in a tree and filling up my water with only the brook to babble with, I felt, though, peaceful and self-reliant.

Then the darkness and night noises crept in to extinguish my calm and brave demeanor along with the last rays of daylight. I was alone and it was dark. Though I have camped and backpacked many nights in my life alone, I have to admit the need this first shady evening to ward off trepidation. I slept fitfully, tossing and turning and would actually have gladly given two granola bars for a snoring bedfellow or two.

So section-hiking off season brought about a new challenge for me - a heightened sense of fear and incredible loneliness. I would hike for weeks and not see or talk to another soul. For a social animal, that is very abnormal. Most of the time, I really enjoyed the solitude (more on that in the gifts chapter), other times I could be so lonesome I literally ached inside for another human being. It wasn't human conversation I missed. I am a single woman and have lived alone, so I am very comfortable with quietness. Besides, the forest is very rarely still.

Morning breaks with the songs of early rising birds, busy chipmunks and chattering squirrels. Hiking, the sounds of my own footsteps cracking a twig, swishing through autumn leaves, thumping along wooden walkways or splashing across a stream keep me company all day long. Daytime birds flitter and flutter and chatter in the canopy, out of sight, but not sound. Nighttime closes with its own melody of night fauna - the hooting of owls, the restful hum of insects and the occasional "what was that?" noise.

Or one may think I would miss human touch the most, especially since I am a very touchy kind of person, coming by it honestly. The Thompson family loves to hug. No matter how often we see each other we always greet one another with a big bear hug with the rule, "Never be the first one to let go in a hug." Arriving or leaving a Thompson abode is like a receiving line at a wedding- lots of hugs! But it was not the sense of touch I longed for the most.

I had plenty of tactile contact with living things walking in the woods. The gentle stroke of a leaf across my check made me feel beloved as I brushed close to a tree. Sometimes the cool fresh morning dew off the foliage would kiss me tenderly with a refreshing assurance. Playful snowballs down my neck from a snow-laden rhododendron, as I stooped under their tunnels of interlocking arms, send shivers down my spine. The splash of icy creek water on my scorching face stimulated me with rejuvenating coolness.

Of course there are endless cruel touches, too. The straps of my heavy backpack rubbed on sore shoulders and hips. Blisters and hot spots on my feet parried for attention in an extreme sensory world enclosed in boots for hours and days. A rock or root, concealed when I set up my tent, would then, after I settled down to a needed night's rest, parade itself under my back, hips and shoulder blades saluting with raised armaments. So no, I was not wanting in the sense of touch.

It is odd; what I missed the most were eyes - those precious windows into another's soul. Seventy percent of our body's sense receptors collect in the eyes! Looking into another life form's eyes is to share pure visual nourishment. So hiking alone in off season I was famished for eye contact. I can remember one section in Massachusetts when the need for countenance was so extreme that I was giddy with joy in playing with a porcupine peeking out from behind the branches of a tree. It had eyes! How I gulped up those big beautiful chestnut-brown eyes that were framed so captivating in clusters of thick dark grayish-black quills tipped in silver and bronze! They were so gorgeous! We connected with one another making goofy expressions around the tree trunk. What fun I had with that lovely-eyed friend!

I never knew how absolute the human need for other life forms was until this experience of days with no living eye contact. Though I have always been an animal lover, both wild and domesticated, I never deeply understood the value of animals to the well-being of humans. Chief Seattle, a respected leader of the Northwestern Indian Nations, spoke these eloquent words in the mid 1850s, "... And what is man without the beasts? If all the beasts were gone, man would die from a great loneliness of spirit..." Oh how true.

There are many touching stories across time and space of the spirits of man and beast connecting. One of my favorites is the tale of Greyfriar's Bobby, a scruffy and shaggy-haired Scottish Terrier and his beloved simple, but kind-hearted human friend, Jock. Several different variations of the story abound, but all agree on the fact that here is an incredible example of loyalty of a dog to a man, even so much that in Edinburgh, Scotland, there is a statue in Greyfriar Square in honor of the little terrier, Bobby.

Some say Jock was Bobby's owner, though homeless like himself; other versions say that Jock befriended the terrier, noticing him wandering the streets and fed him scraps of food that he could hardly spare given his own hunger needs. Whichever, they were inseparable as they roamed the streets of Edinburgh looking for food and shelter each day. When Jock died and was buried in the Kirkyard's cemetery, Bobby followed the gravediggers to where they lay Jock's body. Despite numerous times of being kicked at and rocks thrown at him, for dogs were banned from the churchyard, Bobby snuck back in each time relentlessly.

For fourteen years, day and night, through harsh winter weather and hot summer days, Bobby kept his vigil beside his beloved friend's grave to give tribute to the man that had been kind to him. He left only for brief periods each day to look for food, which he would bring back there to eat. The townspeople were so touched by his loyal and brave watch that they allowed him to live in the cemetery and even erected a small shelter for him beside Jock's grave. When little Bobby died, they buried him alongside the man he had honored with such devotion. There are infinite stories, like Bobby and Jock, of human's bond with animals. How animals enrich our lives and keep us from a "loneliness of spirit."

Even a fictional life form would do at times! Usually at the start of my section hikes, it would take a few days of a beginning mode of fear and over-cautiousness before I found a strength and courage deep inside of me to be out here alone. One particular section, fighting tremors, I climbed up to Catfish Fire Tower in the early autumn morning, after a night of dreaming of mouth-watering pizza and cold refreshing beer. Remember that evening? I was a bit low, still feeling the aftereffects of the torturous vibrations I underwent from neglect at MOC. The incredible views on top, though, were working their magic on my mood. Gazing out in wonder at the canopy covering of a red, gold and orange paisley composition, I noticed some one had left a red wool scarf on the tower's railing.

My trail name of "Dances With Scarf" has incited in me an affinity for scarves. I love them! I am not persnickety about my dancing partner either; any color, fabric and design brings a smile to my face and a skip to my step. But a red wool scarf with a smiling brown eyed Pooh Bear on each end is a delight on any belle's dance card! Frame of mind lifted by that fire tower's view and offering, I danced with Pooh across the miles that day, fantasizing about all the pizza Pooh and I would dine on in the next town we came to. It is remarkable what a tiny, seemingly insignificant, serendipitous gift can do to a girl's disposition in life.

I kept my playful nature alive, though I did not always have a playmate to assuage loneliness. On a particularly hard, though not really grueling, climb up Mt. Everett, I renamed her Mt. Everest, reveling in my strength exhibited. Hiking in an ice storm on Mt. Cube, rather renamed Mt. Ice Cube, I enjoyed playing with the sparkling rainbows in the ice crystals hanging from every tree branch and rock edge. I sat and enjoyed views from bluffs, playing with my shadow.

Besides loneliness, section-hiking off season has logistic challenges as well. Getting to and from each section of the trail you are hiking is expensive and time-consuming. With a thru-hike you only have to do this once at each end. Mass transportation is nonexistent in tiny trail towns, so I had to arrange shuttles from local entrepreneurs or friends that

Playing With my Shadow

lived near the trail corridor. "Cooker-Hiker," living in Maryland, generously offered to do many shuttles and joined me for a few days hiking in some sections. "Harrier," another hiker I had met that '04 summer hike, who lived in Pennsylvania, also offered to do some trail carting around. I also took trains, buses, planes and back of pickup trucks to get to and fro trail segments, always continuously moving northward.

The aforementioned Colemans hosted me in their home and shuttled me to the trail for what was planned to be a three-week section in Pennsylvania in April '05. After a wonderful breakfast of blueberry pancakes at Dan and Pam's home, he drove me to Port Clinton where I resumed the trail where I had gotten off from the last section. Some section-hikers jump all around doing wherever they want and need to fill in their missing pieces of the AT puzzle. But I wanted to keep the continuity of south to north, so I would begin each section where I had ended the time before. So again, waving to a friend and walking into the woods alone, I dueled with my familiar partners of apprehension and autonomy. I should have heeded as an omen for this section, when a boy scout sitting beside me on Pulpit Rock, where his troop had day-hiked to, pulled a huge black snake out from under the rock ledge between my legs. I about peed my pants.

I didn't make it to the planned shelter that night because of those darn rocks. Have I mentioned the famous rocks of Pennsylvania? The trail is littered with them in this state, either small, pointed, gyrating rocks (it is rumored the Pennsylvania Trail Clubs come out at night to sharpen them) or else big slanting, slippery and unstable slabs. It is pure nastiness to feet and leg to walk for miles on these darn rocks. You have to always be looking down, not daring to look up at the view lest you stumble and fall. But it was still a good day; trail magic in the form of surprise food, drink and a lovely sunset topped off the day. I sat up my tent and successfully lassoed a tree with the first throw. Settling in for the night, cozy in my tent I thought to myself, "'Dances with Scarf'", you are one crazy, stubborn and brave woman!"

The next day, trying to see the positive as I grumbled along using my new curse word of rocks, rocks, rocks, I thought at least they keep your mind occupied from thinking about your aches and pains. This day involved a tricky knife edge that scared me and I was really wishing I was not hiking alone. The fear factor is so much greater when you are alone dealing

Rocks of Pennsylvania

with a challenging section of trail. But there were some nice views from the ridges and I was tiptoeing along. At one point the click, click, click of my trekking poles on the rocks and the endless need to carefully place each foot step just so and I thought I would go crazy! Add to this mix miles of broken down trees to climb over and under (hiking early before season, the maintainers have not yet cleared the trails of winter damage). It just wasn't fun out there. If you can believe it, it got worse.

I broke my big toe. Just like I had done a million times over my career of hiking, I stepped from one rock to another, but the second slab moved when I hit it and crushed the foot behind. I was down, my foot painfully trapped between two big rocks. Struggling the pack off, I worked and eased the rock off my foot. Ouch! Resting, regrouping and crying for a few minutes, I cautiously stood to resume hiking,

Rocky Ridge Walk

for the day was wrapping up her lights and I went down again. My foot wouldn't support my weight. I agonizingly took my boot off to assess the injury. Already the toes were turning purple. Well so was the sky so I had to get moving to try and make it to the shelter before dark. I did not want the added chore of setting up my tent. Arriving as the last rays of light cast their glow through the trees, I didn't even make dinner but spread out my bag and laid down. Spirits are low as I try to get comfortable so the relief of sleep will come.

I awoke the next morning to a painfully swollen, purple, puss-filled, blistered bent toe that was the ugliest thing I have ever seen in my life. I think Amy, "Nails" daughter, who was kind enough to come and get me at Wind Gap that next evening where I bailed out, would agree. But first there is 4.6 of the most, the very most, excruciating and painful miles I have ever lived through. Putting my boot back on that morning, a stick in my mouth like I had seen done in the Westerns when they were amputating a leg with no anesthetic, I almost passed out. Oddly and well-timed, this was the only section of trail that I allowed my family to talk me into bringing a cell phone. I was of the belief that they didn't belong out here in nature. But my hiking alone was worrying folks back home so I pacified them. That morning, I called family and lined up my closest geographically member, well my sister "Nails'" closest loved one, her daughter, Amy, who lived a few hours away to come and get me and take me back to Dan and Pam's where my car was. Amy's kindness will forever be treasured.

The AT had beat me. My web site letter to my supportive friends and family after this section read: "I am off the trail for good. Why? Broken toe, broken blow down trees, and broken spirit...The rock climbing required on the northern half of the AT is just beyond my skill and comfort level. But you know there has been a surprising gift received in this experience for me. It is quite humbling and makes me smile inside to realize - yes there are mountains greater and wilder than me... I will not hike any more on the AT. Thanks for all your support of my hike. Love, "'Dances With Scarf.'"

Responses to my letter and vow to quit filled my dilapidated spirit: "...A mountain wilder than you?! Hard for me to imagine..." and "I certainly don't think that the need to concede that there are moun-tains too rocky for you to climb is in any way a defeat and I KNOW that the only thing broken about you is your toe, for your spirit is unbreakable." "You have one of the Largest Spirits I know of - right now it may be a little scarred, but it's not broken. And your spirit will heal- and maybe you'll try again and maybe not- but you need to know what you did do is awesome - you are a Great Mountain Woman!"

Well I reckon friends and family know me better than I do myself, for November 1, 2005 I was back at Wind Gap waving goodbye to Harrier walking into those blasted woods again following white blazes to Maine. Yes, I do have a cocky attitude now, for if Lehigh Gap and broken toes didn't beat me, nothing can! I met my first SOBO (south bounder - hiking from Maine to Georgia, only about 25% of thru-hikers do this direction) today; Preacher Bob and I chatted for a bit about Jesus and C.S. Lewis. Later, sitting by Sunfish Pond luxuriating in the fall colors reflecting in the lake, I shared my bench with a gentleman day-

She's Back!

hiker, coming up just as far on the trail as to this pond, then turning around. As I got up to move on, he said, "Hey, what's your name?" I was taken aback a bit, knowing I'd probably never see the man again since we were heading in opposite directions. So what difference did it make for him to know my name, but I politely answered, "Karen," giving my given name for some reason instead of my usual response on the AT of my trail name. Then he genuinely added, "I just wanted to add you to my prayer list." I sure prefer these powerful omens over last year's snake flanked by my two shaking legs! Now this section-hike is gonna be good. I just know it! There are still some lingering lovely fall colors and the temperatures are in the 60's during the day. Oh yeah! It was a perfect hike!

Hiking in April '06 in the north, where winter still lingers on, I am alone 95% of the time during this section-hike, too. Easter weekend there were a few souls out celebrating the season by walking in the woods. So that Saturday evening I shared a shelter after being alone for eight days straight. "Stops for Berries" from New York was a delightful and jolly fellow. He built an awesome fire but I was too cold to crawl out of my sleeping bag to get nearer its warmth so just watched from a distance. Even away from its instant heat, the glowing flames dancing around against the dark background warmed my spirit in a different way. Conversation with a fellow hiker added warmth as well.

This cordiality was well-needed for the next day was rough climbing Glastenbury Mountain in deep snow. These are really not safe conditions to be hiking in, especially alone. But there is no easy out at this point. I am not near a road so I unwisely head over Stratton Mountain which is clothed in deep snow and icy patches. During the warmth of the day the sun melts the snow then night freezes it again and makes for very greasy conditions between the layers and me. There were beautiful views on top of Stratton, making the arduous and slippery climb up worth it. The brilliant blue sky elevated my attitude as well as my eyes as they were drawn upward to gaze. How blessed we are to live in a world with colored skies!

I remember researching my three-year-old child's ageless question of, "Momma, why is the sky blue?" Simply put, the sun's white light is actually a spectrum of six colored rays. When this spectrum collides with earth's gaseous atmosphere, made up of atoms of primarily oxygen and nitrogen, along with particles of dust and moisture, blue light, being the most active light of the observable spectrum, is scattered all over the sky. To my inquisitive three-year-old's brain (and my own for that matter) who cannot possibly conceive this science, I'd just say, "Maybe it was God's favorite color to paint with so He wanted to use a lot of blue, like you do with red paint, so He painted the big sky blue!" Then we'd lay in the grass and ponder what the sky would be like if it was another color. Today hiking over difficult terrain in dangerous conditions, I was very thankful of a gift of blue sky to help ward off the coldness of loneliness.

Gifts and Rewards

"We need sometimes that poetry should not be droned into our ears, but flashed into our senses. And man, with all his knowledge and pride, needs sometimes to know nothing and feel nothing but that he is a marvelous atom in a marvelous world."
Laura and Guy Waterman

Besides lovely blue skies, the AT gave me so many gifts and rewards showing me afresh what a marvelous world we live in! I have already celebrated greatly in earlier chapters the incredible kindness of fellow hikers and town folks that warmed my heart so much. Gifts of natural beauty enriched my soul as well- sunrises, sunsets, wildlife, trees of every hue and shape, mist, bubbling brooks and endless other treats of nature. All my life I have enjoyed and appreciated the out-of-doors, but walking through four distinct seasons across a continent was so amazingly enriching. Completely experiencing the changing forest as she blended from one to another showed me an approach of gracefulness and acceptance at my own flow through the seasons of life. This journey taught me other noble lessons such as the peace and happiness of living simply and the art of living in the present moment. I learned to appreciate so many things that I had taken for granted or had not noticed enough in my "other" life. When I resumed the trail as a section-hiker, hiking alone endowed me with the gift of solitude and an opportunity to meditate as I walked, bringing me closer to God than I have ever been in my life.

Time with God/Solitude

"Pray without ceasing."
                    I Thessalonians 5:17

*"Oh! I have slipped the surly bonds of earth...put
out my hand and touched the face of God."*
                    John G. Magee, Jr.

I was always so ecstatic to be back on the trail
during my two to six weeks section-hikes, continuing
pursuing my dream. Oh how I do love these white
blazes. I touch them every once in awhile with rever-
ence; I am in awe that a footpath exists like this for
over 2000 miles through the mountains. It was a bit
sad though to not meet my familiar "trail family"
snack breaking at the next lovely overlook or cooking
their various meals at the shelters. But as much as I

Me and my Beloved AT White Blazes

loved hiking with "Nails" and the rest of my "family" and truly prefer the joy of her companionship to aloneness, hiking alone had its own gifts.

After I disposed of the initial creeping in of fears and adjusted to the hushed stillness, my independent nature kicked in. I learned to enjoy and appreciate the solitude. I had time for introspection, observation and holy communion with God. I talked and listened to God all day. I stayed in complete awe of His creation.

I have been labeled a Pantheist because of how I worship God through an appreciation of nature, His creation. I never understood the difference in praising the Creator or His Creation. Aren't they one in the same? Don't we stare with admiration at "Starry Night," simultaneously marveling at Van Gogh's handiwork? Don't we gaze with awe at Michelangelo's frescoes in the Sistine Chapel, praising both the masterpiece and the master artist? But I am not concerned by this categorization of my spirituality; I just know I always feel closest to God in nature. Now hiking alone, without sharing my focus on a society of fellow hikers, I attended "Church" more.

For me there is no grander sanctuary than dawn on a mountain top that reaches toward heaven, with the morning mist rising in the valley below as the choir of birds sing praises to the resurrected sun. No cathedral is more stunning than a forest with sunshine streaming in golden columns among the raised boughs of sun-worshiping trees. A refreshing drink of cold mountain stream water or the lusciousness of wild blueberries eaten on a rock outcrop is pure and holy communion with God. Hiking on the

AT alone gave me this magnificent of all gifts- being with God.

I walked, praying unceasingly. As a child this was always my favorite Bible verse - "Pray without ceasing." Maybe it was much loved then because it was short enough for me to memorize easily. But no, I think it went deeper than that for me even at that young age or maybe because of that fresh age of innocence, when I could believe I could live my life in this way - praying perpetually. I have continued to this day to try to do just that and when practiced it is a beautiful attitude for life and especially powerful in strenuous situations like long distance hiking. It most certainly carried me more gracefully and gratefully over the Appalachian Trail.

I do admit though, that not only did God get the credit for every breathtaking view, each cool sip of water and welcomed shelter around the bend, He also got blame for rainy day on top of rainy day, body and legs weary to the bone marrow and miles that stretched farther than my feet could measure. But whether "bad" or "good," rain or shine, pain or joy, it was an incredible gift to have this time to talk with God.

Natural Delights

*"Every object, every being, is a jar full of delight.
Be a connoisseur."*

Rumi

Did you know that pine cones are architecturally perfected for capturing wind from any direc-

God's Incredible Handiwork

tion so that they can catch life abiding pollen from the passing breezes? They are turbine shaped with petal blades that cause air to spin immediately above them, but the still air down in the cone welcomes the spinning pollen as it falls into the waiting calm petals. It is completely incredible how every tiny aspect of nature is superlatively designed! How can one not believe in God! I have always been an avid nature lover and connoisseur of its delights from the tiniest seed to the immeasurable night sky. This was the original lure of my dream of hiking the AT - time exploring and living in nature through each of her wondrous seasons.

Each season has inherent tests to endure, as noted before and wonderful bequests to enjoy. I had the delight of experiencing all four - winter, spring, summer and autumn - on the Appalachian Trail. Starting the trail on the last day of February and then hiking sections in mid November and early April, I experienced much more of winter than any other season. I gazed enthralled at the Christmas card scenes in front of me. I danced and frolicked with snowflakes. Ice palaces shimmered on mountaintops and I was queen for the day in this magical wonderland. I played with the rhododendron tunnels in the southern part of the AT. It is easy for a childlike attitude to overcome you hiking through these canopies. With snow on them they were especially lovely and playful, throwing snowballs down your back as you went under them.

Hiking in the winter season gave me many beautiful views that I would not have seen with the canopy of leaves up. To stand on top of a mountain or ridge and look out at our earth's landscape is pure ecstasy! Ridge walking, I would gaze down into valleys where I supposed that "normal" people were going about their ordinary day. Not that I could see these specks of action of course at my elevation, but I pondered it walking along, feeling so different, cut-off from my society of humans and the "norm." Sometimes I would feel oddly empowered to have broken away, if just for a bit, free from the boredom of daily monotony. Other times, the scene would draw me down and I would feel incredibly lonely, so separated from my fellow specie that I longed to be simply hanging clothes out on a line in the wind to dry or driving a winding country road to the security of a job routine in town. At night, I could see dots of homey lights scattered over the dark valley floor like sparkling jewels upon a sea of black velvet. Again this brought conflicting feelings - one of enchantment, the other of discontent. One particular early winter evening I wrote in my journal as I was gazing down at the lights in the valley below, "They are warm. I am not..." It was odd; these views were almost dreamlike. Maybe it was because the landscape around me was all so still and I, alone, moved through it dreamlike.

A unique view on the trail at Mombasha High Point in New York, was far away in the distance I could see the New York City skyline! It was very surreal; I agree with "Nails'" description of it, "It looks like Dorothy's first view of OZ." Surprisingly, New York City, at its closest, is only 34 miles by road from the trail. In fact on the trail near Pawling, New York, is the Appalachian Trail Railroad Station– a small platform where you can actually catch the train into the monstrosity of New York City, if you are game for a "culture shock!" Joined by friend and fellow hiker "Cooker Hiker," we rode the rails into the big city spending

Train Station on the AT Going to New York City

Central Park – New York City

a delightful day exploring the concrete and glass man-made corridors and delicious ethnic restaurants. What a hoot; what a contrast! He laughed, though, at my answer to his question of what was my favorite thing about the metropolis. "Central Park!" I answered, for I loved the meandering paths, giant sprawling trees and picnickers in the smooth green lawns of Central Park.

Spring brought reviving rain and warmth encouraging life to blossom in the woods. Despite the groaning I did earlier regarding rain, I want to also include it in the gifts chapters, for yes hiking in rain is difficult, but there is also a subtle beauty in a forest washed afresh by rain. The leaves glisten from their bath. Bent over from the weight of the scrubbing I would notice an angle, veins or a side and color of the leaf I had never seen before. In a winter rain the tones in the woods are every imaginable hue of gray that lies between black and white. In spring and summer rains, the moisture deepens the greens to differing shades depending on their initial color and the medium of the leaf itself. Undergrowth and flowers bow their perky heads in humility to rain's weight. The smells are of rich humus and fresh life. The spring greening of the woods is a miracle to behold.

The swishing of my nylon rain pants and squeak of my saturated hiking boots and socks war for my focus with the rain's crescendo of pitter patters. The deafening roar, if it is a hard rain, is the only sound in your head, its beat even drowning thoughts. Swollen creeks are heard before seen. The sounds, smells and sights of rain in the forest lift both my mind and body to a strangely ethereal plane. I like to hike in this rainy world, for awhile...

Summer on the Trail

It was a summer day to celebrate when it was warm enough to finally wear shorts. Bending legs miles upon miles is easier without the compounding drag of also lifting material with each step. Cooler evenings required zipping "legs" back on the pants which would look stylish for they were clean and the top shorts were dirty. The year 2004 was the summer for the seventeen year cicadas. They were absolutely deafening in the woods and even their little discarded exoskeletons would noisily crunch beneath my feet as I walked the path.

Summer seems to encourage play. On top of Unaka Mountain, in Tennessee, I entered an unexpected red spruce forest, more typical of the northern woods, I thought. Middle Earth-like, I anticipated having lunch with a gnome or hobbit or Tolkien himself. I crawled in and amongst the limbs hiding and looking for playmates. Other pleasurable summer pals are water bodies – creeks, ponds and rivers. Rivers snake their path through valleys below, showing a bend of their body for a turn then hiding from view only to reappear again around the next curve of the trail, like a shadow playing with moving clouds and a lazy sun.

The trail crosses some of the greatest rivers of the east: the Nantahala and French Broad in North Carolina; Pigeon and Nolichucky in Tennessee; Holston-Middle and North Forks, New and James in Virginia; Shenandoah and Potomac in West Virginia; Susquehanna, Schuylkill, Lehigh and Delaware in Pennsylvania; Hudson in New York; Housatonic and Hoosic in Massachusetts; Winhall, White and Connecticut in Vermont; Rattle and Androscoggin in New Hampshire;

Delaware River

South Branch of Carabassett, Kennebec, West and East Branch of Piscataquis, East Branch of Pleasant and West Branch of Penobscot in Maine. Seeing these rivers first winding below you as a thread in the distance, coming closer and closer until finally you cross its wide strand is verification of your mobility across these mountain ranges. I am truly walking across a continent. Also these noble and historic rivers of the Appalachian Range connected me with my forefathers and I felt one with the early pioneers that walked this country. Rivers were so important in the creation of this land— life-giving water, food, transportation and trade. How humankind's lives have been formed around and by these great rivers. I had the rare privilege, viewing them from the wild mountains that embraced them, to behold them as the first settlers would have, unencumbered by mankind's clutter. For me they beautifully bridged not only past to present but linked the many inter-ruptions of my goal of continuity south to north. I loved these rivers with all the hearts of humankind past and present.

The sections I hiked in November were some-times still ablaze with fall colors. On one absolutely perfect blue sky autumn day with ideal tempera-tures I was glad to be alive and hiking. A pastoral setting of eight easy miles walking through Cumber-land Valley in Pennsylvania had me joyfully strolling along taking inward the wholesome scene around me. A panorama of farm buildings, silos, rustic weathered barns, white church steeples pointing heavenward, big white farmhouses with wraparound porches draped with comfy porch swings and vivid fall flowers and crops in the fields bronzed with the abundance of harvest filled my heart with the goodness of clean and hard-working honest folks. To put the last touches on

Pastoral Panorama

this idyllic picture onto my mind and in my heart forever, I heard a distant church chime playing "The Old Rugged Cross." I felt truly blessed.

Blessing of Simplicity

"The simpler you make things, the richer the experience."
Steve House

One of the greatest lessons the AT taught me was the purity, peace and happiness found in simplicity. It is truly an amazing revelation to realize how very little we really need in life. On the trail all I really needed was food, water, shelter and a privy. How simple is that? Anything else was a special treat – icing on the cake or an apple for lunch. I love apples. At home I enjoy an apple a day, but apples are heavy, therefore not a good backpacking item. Leaving a trail town, I would sometimes treat myself and carry an apple for first break (we always eat the heaviest food items in our pack first). I didn't enjoy those special apples; I simply and purely delighted in them – scrumptious, luscious bite after scrumptious, luscious bite.

Food out of the ordinary hiker fare is the ultimate treat. In Shenandoah National Park at park waysides, just a short detour from the trail, you can buy cheese-burgers and in season, which it was when I was there, blackberry milkshakes. Yummy!! Cold, fruity, dairy, caloric – what more could I need? Other hiker's food always looked better to me than my own, well except for Ramen noodles. I got so extremely tired of my food that sometimes I just couldn't even force myself to eat though starving.

"Nails" loves to tell a few stories on me of "foods"

Enjoying a Simple Apple

I consumed that I normally would try to avoid at all costs. My first odd meal was while we were resting at a shelter on a lunch break. I was mixing in my water an envelope of "Emer'gen-C," a fizzing energy booster drink, when in went an uninvited wee little guest. Noticing it, I stuck my finger in my cup, caught the little bugger and proceeded to suck him off my finger. She burst out laughing, while I, perplexed at myself, wondered why I had done such a silly thing. My only defense is fatigue. I just didn't think.

The other occasion I did think and decided being an appreciative guest was more important than keeping to my healthy diet lifestyle. We were at Tillie's Wood's Hole Hostel a few weeks before her usual season to host hikers, but being the gracious lady she was (she passed away October 2007) she didn't turn us away. Apologizing at breakfast for the meager fare, for she hadn't done her shopping yet, she made us from her pantry store, pancakes and fried spam. My lips hadn't touched spam (an acronym we came up with is "specially prepared animal matter") for centuries - yuk! But I wouldn't think of hurting her feelings by refusing, though I did decline a second helping to her perplexed look, for hikers never turn down second helpings of food. For Christmas the following year, "Nails" gave me a Spam Cookbook full of delectable ways to prepare this "meat." Sorry, "Nails," it went to Goodwill.

Wood's Hole - Tillie's Place

Water- delicious cold spring water - there is nothing on the planet more refreshing! Ardently the next water source is anticipated when hiking not so much for survival, thirst or re-hydration, though of course those reasons are paramount, but for the pure ecstasy of simple cold mountain water. The font of the next water source was as precious news to us as awaiting the announcement of the sex of a newborn baby - girl or boy? Spring or creek or pond? Just as a parent is blissful with either, so is a thirsty and hot hiker. Not only does water quench our thirst and ardor, but it also soothes and cleans weary, hot and blistered feet, itchy legs, sultry face and neck. Many a time did I dip my famed scarf into a cold brook to wrap around my forehead, the coolness fueling me up that next mountain. I remember one spring in particular in Virginia called Ginger Spring; the water was delectable! The finest wine in Italy could not have tasted better. There were many springs and creeks with delicious and refreshing water. Water - how very exquisite a treat it is. For the rest of my days, I will appreciate and relish a drink of water with a whole new depth and awe. It is life giving.

Another glorious attribute of water is that of cleaning one's body with it. Never will I not feel

Glorious Life-giving Water

gratitude and joy for a hot shower again!!! AHHH–HHHHH.......The desire and need for a shower would began getting very strong about day four or five from the last one. Once, though only on day two, I indulged in a hot shower in the middle of the woods. A mirage, I first thought, seeing the sign at Dahlgren Back Pack Campground in Maryland for hot showers. Though it had only been 48 hours since my last bath, I couldn't resist. I mean it's a HOT shower.

Home Sweet Home – AT Shelter

Shelter at day's end is looked forward to as much as a barn at trail's end for a tired horse. Though only simple three sided rough wood or stone structures with hard plank floors they still feel like a five-star hotel. Utterly exhausted from walking and my pack biting into sore shoulders at day's end, I anticipate relief around every bend. When the shelter comes into view, a relieved sigh swells my chest as I plop my pack down on the board's edge grateful to stop at my "home" for the night. Before relaxing, I lay out my bed roll, fill and treat water bottles, fix dinner, hang my food bags up in the trees away from hungry coons, bears and mice, and lastly visit the privy.

Then tucking myself into my sleeping bag and saying my evening prayers, I could finally just be there. Most of the time I would lay there thinking of the day or listen with pleasure to the mysterious night sounds, but sometimes I would tense with paranoid imaginings of what was in the forest out to get me, unable to fall into needed sleep. Minds are powerful imaginers and fatigue breeds uncertainties and fears. In the morning light I would laugh, although grudging the lack of a good night's sleep, at these misgivings and rebuke myself for such fearful and ridiculous negativity. But at night they seemed so very real. The majority of the time though the shelters gave me a sense of security, despite the actuality of their vulnerability.

Ahh - a good clean privy- what more could a girl want? There are all types and designs of interesting outhouses at the shelters on the trail - the typical carved out moon on the door, solar fanned, women and men's (how frivolous!), curtained windows, two-seaters with a cribbage board between the holes and privies with a view. Always a respectable distance from the shelter and water source, privies ranged from rough to swanky. Despite the usual residents evidenced by cobwebs over head and small droppings on the seat and floor, cold air whipping up through the hole to freeze the buns and minimal toilet paper, they were still greatly appreciated for without them

A Little Privacy in the Privy, Please!

was the added chore of digging a cat hole for bodily wastes.

Once, definitely only once, I did a work trade-for-stay in an AMC fee-required shelter in New Hampshire. After hiking twelve difficult miles that day, my assigned "job," in lieu of the twelve dollar nightly shelter fee, was to go through the privy's waste and pick out the items that were not biodegradable - an extremely cruel and yukky charge, I felt! Though I am most certainly an eco-friendly kinda gal, this is one "green" duty I will refuse, no pun intended, to do again. It did bring to mind, in quite vivid sensory awareness, a short but profound message I remembered learning in a college environmental course; there is no "away" in throw away. Everything ends up somewhere.

Living in the Present Moment

> "The way to get there is to be there."
> <u>Conversations with God</u>

> "When the flower opens, the bees will come."
> Kabir

For years it has been a challenge, though a heart-felt aspiration of mine to learn to practice the art of living in the present moment. Many of my prayers, rituals and meditations have the intention to nurture this teaching. But it always seemed to be an inner struggle for me to train my mind and heart to not look back or ahead. How we lose the joy of the moment in living in that way. I have had a cartoon on my frig for decades of two children sitting in the grass with the little girl saying to her friend wisely, "Yesterday's the past, tomorrow's the future, but today is a gift. That's why it's called the present." Yeah....

Walking on a trail like the picture on the opposite page, one has no choice but to live in the now! Ouch! With many such situations in walking the Appalachian Trail, truly and finally I have learned to live in present moment, for the "gift" of the present is persistently underfoot. Not only in regard to safety, but also an incessant awareness awakens your senses to the beauty that surrounds you or the pains within

Necessity of Living in Present Moment

you. Immersed in this linear world of a path in the woods, it becomes your whole existence. Your focus is not in competition with a dozen other divergences as it is in the normal world. I noticed every slight thing as I hiked - a little striped chipmunk scurrying along a half-rotten log, the play of sunbeams on frosted leaf edges, the gurgling brook choosing varying paths as it leaped, frothy over mossy rocks and tickled tree roots at water's edge, mint or herbal smells, warm vacuums of air stirring in low hollows and calls of birds announcing my disturbance to their province of winged subjects. I finally learned to live in the now on the AT and I have carried that awareness back with me to my normal world. I open each "gift" of today in rich presence. Whether wrapped in joy or sorrow, I am there in the unveiling, conscious and grateful.

Especially Special Moments

> "How we spend our days is, of course, how we spend our lives..."
>
> Annie Dillard

The trail had so many "presents" of deep worth that cause inhales of satisfying breaths that reach my soul and lodge there forever, but some stand out above all the others. One such special moment that I hold dear in my heart and mind was on Max Patch, a grassy top mountain of 4,629 feet, in North Carolina in late March. As I mentioned before, women are a minority on the trail. This special evening it

Me, "Nails" and "Hippie Longstocking" on Max Patch, N.C.

McAfee Knob in Virginia

just worked out that camped on this beautiful bald
with panoramic views all the way around of layer
after layer of undulating mountains were three solo-
hiking women - "Nails," "Hippie Longstocking" and
me. Our tents were similar and the picture of us by
our individual tents with ridges of mountains in the
background is forever imprinted on my heart. We
had a lovely evening sharing stories, a meal and a
sunset. Those three tents in the grassy meadow on
top of a mountain should have been on the cover of
Backpacker Magazine. The only dark cloud on that
bald was I thought I had lost my scarf. I found it at
daybreak the next morning and gleefully yelled across
to "Nails'" tent, "I found it! I found it!" waving it out
my tent door. "Nails'" later told me that is a picture
she will always have in her mind - the orange sunrise
over the farthest mountain ridge and me sticking my
head and arm out of the tent waving my scarf in the
morning mist with a smile in my voice.

McAfee Knob, in central Virginia, was another

amazing place. Perched on that rock overhanging, taking in big breaths of wholesome air and gazing out at the mountains and valleys, I felt so alive and at one with the world. In the distance I could see Tinker Cliffs, where I would hike the next day. It struck me anew each time I could see where I had just walked or where I would tomorrow, how incredible walking this trail was. Putting a landscape together picture after picture into a whole earth is a neat venture.

I spent my 47th birthday on the trail. That May 9th day, I walked a section of the trail that was covered with bouquets of spring wildflowers - mayapples, lady slippers, jack-in-the-pulpits, trilliums - to help me celebrate my own birth of life. I camped the eve of my birthday in a patch of trillions of trilliums. It was magical! The next morning "Nails" airmailed me a lovely birthday card sailing from my tent to hers over the pink heads perking up for the day. I had

My Birthday Shared With Trilliums on the Trail

a Snickers candy bar cake with a candle on it that evening in the shelter.

Small natural offerings can miraculously alter a weary body, mind and spirit. Hiking an extremely long 20.6 mile day in a cold rain on an April section-hike in Massachusetts, then hiking an extra half of a mile that felt like ten on a side trail, only to find the promised rare four-sided shelter of Upper Goose Pond Cabin closed due to the early time of year, was dreadfully disheartening. Being nothing I could do about my situation, I set to my evening tasks in a

Pond in Evening Mist

gray fog. I laid out my sleeping bag on the thankfully covered at least porch, made dinner, hung my food bag, then headed to the pond to get water. With the mist clinging lovingly to the water's surface and the gray silhouettes of trees and rocks hugging the pond's oval frame, Upper Goose Pond was purely exquisite. Still, though surrounded by such beauty or maybe because of it and the basic human need to share such perfection aching in my heart, I was feeling lonely as hell standing at the silent pond's edge. The single soft dipping sound of my water bottle into the mysterious liquid element accented my aloneness. Then out of the gray fog toward me, pure instant vivacity bigger than life itself, flew a flock of geese. Their jubilant quacking and joyful splashy landing on the water directly in front of me completely shifted the melancholy scene to that of euphoric happiness. Friends had arrived to share the beauty and magic of the evening with me! Their ruckus in the water as they playfully bathed and splashed woke other birds from their own dismal tempers, so from dripping bough beds all around the pond came gleeful songs of dusk time play. I slept warm and dry on my porch divan with gratefulness in my heart and joy embossed on my face, while my new-found feathered friends, heads tucked into their own dry, warm fluff, stood at the pond's edge as watchful sentinels of gray moods.

"Work-for-Stay" at Lakes of the Clouds Hut

The AMC Huts in the White Mountains are very interesting and a unique treat. "Hut" is not quite the correct term to call these classy accommodations for it implies a much more rustic shelter than these are. Run by the Appalachian Mountain Club they are large, enclosed structures with full services of wonderful hot meals, bedded bunks, indoor bathrooms and entertaining evening programs. They allow AT thru and section-hikers to "work-for-stay," since they are a bit pricy for our gypsy budgets. But you get two hot meals and a bed in exchange for a bit of work. So "Nails" and I donned our aprons and washed dishes in the kitchen of the Lakes of the Clouds Hut along with "Mountain Goat" and "Firefly." It was fun! We ate with the regular crew and slept on the tables in the dining hall that night, rising before breakfast to help with the morning meal before we headed north on the trail to climb the famous Mt. Washington!

Mt. Washington is famous for many reasons. At 6288 feet, it is the highest peak in New England and was the mountain originally proposed to be the northern terminus of the AT by Benton MacKaye in 1921. It has an obnoxious road to the top, loathsome at least to weary hikers that climbed the mountain using foot, not horse power (okay maybe the resentment is also fueled a bit by jealousy). Cars receive a bumper sticker saying, "This car climbed Mt. Washington." Ha! The summit has a weather station that has clocked the highest official surface wind speed (231 MPH) ever recorded on earth. At the Visitor Center on the top you can read about all the lives that mountain claims every year and eat hot food at the snack bar there. We took our pictures in the fog

Summit of Mt. Washington

and wind holding on to the sign at the summit.

Leaving the summit we heard the whistle of the Mt. Washington Cog Train, the oldest such railway in the world, which has been chugging visitors up to the top of the mountain since 1869. AT hikers have a tradition of mooning the cog train as it goes by in rebellion for their easy ride up and down as opposed to our hike up. I laughed and said, "But really are we actually going to do it?" when "Nails" suggested we keep to the tradition and moon the train. "It's tradition," "Nails" playfully argued. I think the train staff and riders were also aware of the AT custom for when they saw us, the engineer blew the whistle and all the passengers posed at the windows with their cameras ready and directed at us. Geez, I hope none of them had close up lenses! So turning our backsides to the train, dropping our packs and our drawers we mooned the cog train, laughing so hard my jaws hurt. Our daughters, when told, replied, "Great.... now our mom's butts are going to be on the internet!" Well no one will recognize them as ours, will they?

Noticing a marker to a side trail, I almost passed it by, for I rarely do extra mileage down alternate

Cog Train on Mt. Washington

trails, when catching my breath, I whispered reverently "Katahdin..." for the sign said "to view of Mt. Katahdin." We ran, the first time to do thus and arriving at the end of the short side trail we looked around not seeing any BIG mountains at first glance. Then as we completed our circumnavigation there she was - wham! She took up the whole sky; she was so near! I got very emotional as I saw my first close-up sight of this mountain I had been walking toward for almost six months and over 2000 miles. I could see individual flanks, shoulders and crests. "Nails" and I both cried sitting there looking at our goal, for the first time believing it was reachable. Then we got silly, as we practiced our summit poses with Mt. Katahdin smiling over our shoulder in the background. We were

First Close-up View of Mt. Katahdin

completely giddy with joy! What has been for thousands of miles some magical mountain way up north
is now right in front of me. In just a few days my feet
will touch Mt. Katahdin- the "greatest mountain."

Milestones

> "Yearn for something. As long as you yearn,
> you can't congeal; there is a forward motion to
> yearning."
>
> Gail Godwin

Milestones such as state lines, the big "OOO" mile-
ages and memorable landmarks are just cause for
great motivation and celebration. After the painful
realization sets in early that Mt. Katahdin is really a
long way off, one needs attainable goals that don't
feel impossible to reach. These smaller and more

manageable motivating objectives help to keep me moving. I will mention a few of the more special ones that I have not mentioned before.

State Lines – N.Y and N.J

Wow! I have walked 1000 miles today, my 88th day on the trail! At the 1000 mile mark, or near enough as we could tell in the middle of the woods, "Nails" and I, not having any bubbly champagne nor flutes in which to properly celebrate this accomplishment, toasted with the end of our water hoses. Amazing - 1000 miles! Even without the sparkling wine, we were still bubbly the rest of the day.

When I crossed the Vermont State line, my

twelfth state, I gleefully yelled to Howard Duncan in Tennessee, "I am in Vermont, Howard!" He was in on this hike when I first began turning a dream into a plan. He shares my vision of hiking the entire Appalachian Trail and I am sure he, too, will complete it someday. But way back then when we'd wonder and fantasize about hiking the trail, it seemed it wasn't Maine that was our ultimate high castle in the sky, but Vermont. The kingdom of Vermont just sounded so north and exotic when sitting at our desks at work in Tennessee.

Maine! Reaching that state was the first time I allowed myself to believe I would finish the Appalachian Trail! But after only fifteen minutes of being in that long anticipated state, I had changed her name to "Maim." First I had an "out of my comfort zone" rope-aided rock climb where I scraped my knees up badly so blood was pouring down my leg. Then at another rock scramble I ripped the whole back out of my pants - my only pair of pants. I was apologizing to every one I met for the extra "view" they were getting in Maine! I had days and miles before I came to a town with stores. A few days later in Full Goose Shelter, full of not quacking geese but college kids out for a weekend jaunt, one kid took pity on me or maybe on everybody else and gave me his extra pair of shorts which I wore under my pants till I got to the next town.

This all happened before we even got to the long talked about and dreaded "Mahoosuc Notch"- the meanest mile on the trail! This one-mile long rock and boulder, on knees or butt, crawl/scramble is reputed

Maine State Line

to have ice in some of the crevices where the sun never shines up into August! To "welcome" us there was a dead and decaying moose laying on the trail at the beginning of the notch (cause of death contro-versial). We had heard about his death through the trail vine. I began smelling it a half of a mile before we reached him; the stench made my throat gag and my stomach heave. I had to step right over his rotting body. It was touching though for someone had hung Buddhist prayer flags in the trees above him. It took us three and one-half hours to go that one mile and it was a hoot! Teamwork between "Nails" and me included pulling and pushing each other up, over and under rocks. Packs off, packs on, packs off/on was exhausting but an amusing adventure!

Kennebec River in Maine is an exciting and interesting northern landmark. It is dangerous to ford because the water level can rise and surge at any time due to water being released at a dam upstream whenever power generation is needed. A section-hiker drowned here in 1985 trying to ford; since then a ferry service was installed during peak hiking season. It is the only river on the AT that the ATC services a free canoe ferry across the river at scheduled hours. Leaving our warm beds in plenty of time to meet the ferry we were excited about the novelty of this official AT route sitting down in a canoe. Standing on the bank of the sparkling blue water my spirits were high- the Kennebec River! Dave Corrigan, the ferryman, graciously loaded our packs in the canoe, and with a hand to aid us in we sat down and were

Ferryman Dave Rowing Across the Kennebec River in Maine

Katahdin - 14.8 Miles!

rowed across this unique section of "trail."

Hiking the entire AT uses a set of forty-two maps. When I unfolded map # 1 (they are numbered north to south) I simply cried. Oh my goodness - map # 1; I am almost done! What had seemed almost impossible was within reach. In the dreaming stage, I remember all those maps spread all over my floor and over an impossible territory to think of actually walking over. I remember reverently holding the last one with Katahdin on it and wondering/hoping that someday I would unfold that map and be there. That day is here; all day I had to keep unfolding my map just to look at it in disbelief. Mt. Katahdin - the end. As the signage on the trail started listing the distance to the end - the last mountain - in the teens I was numb with wonderment. To comprehend that it was only 14.8 miles to Mt. Katahdin and the finish of my dream hike of 2174.1 miles was impenetrable to my mind, body and heart.

The Finale - Summit Day

It's good to have an end to journey toward, but it is the journey that matters in the end."

Ursula K. LeGuin

"Let the beauty we love be what we do. There are hundreds of ways to kneel and kiss the ground."

Rumi

Tomorrow I climb Mt. Katahdin. Tomorrow I finish the Appalachian Trail and fulfill a lifelong dream. There are no words to express how I feel this evening as I lay awake too excited to sleep, in the shelter at the base of that great mountain. I have to admit to opposing feelings - amazing relief intermingling with sorrowful regret with the realization that my hike will soon be over. A goal I have been walking toward for over three years and thousands of miles is in my reach. What then? What next?

Waking up at 5:00 AM on summit day, checking the weather, I am elated for we have a Class I Weather Day! The report read for temperatures in the 70s, clear blue sky, no rain in the forecast and calm winds which is the very best, the most perfect wished-for day for our finale of this amazing journey. We are on the trail by 6 AM and start the ascent of an elevation gain of 4177 feet in 5.2 miles which translates as one steep up hill climb, but our last! I am now hiking with the power of many such climbs stored in my bones and spirit; my feet this day have a life of their own. It is strange to watch the peak to our left as I gaze over my shoulder, that at the start of the climb had seemed so monstrous, as only a bump on the ground. I am climbing this greatest mountain-strong and sure.

The Tableland on top is so lovely - alpine scenery with colors of rust, bronze, bright green and silver-gray. Passing Thoreau Spring - a place that I had read about for years was fantastic. Then the summit sign - the damn sign... the sign I have been dreaming of since I was ten years old! Tears streaming down my elated face, "Nails" and I walked together to the sign and fell against it and cried. We did it! I did it!

Standing by that sign I just couldn't even grasp that I was really here on top of the Mt. Katahdin. I did my last dance with my battered green paisley scarf, tears of joy, gratefulness and relief still falling. I prayed, thanking God for this experience. I soaked up the positive and high energy of that special place. We stayed on top of Mt. Katahdin for over an hour, relishing our well-deserved fame and this amazing day. Gazing at the incredible 360 degree views, I sat there in an aura of disbelief that it is done. Rich, waiting below for us, later told us he was concerned about us taking so long so he was asking folks coming back down if they had seen us. Several replied, "Are they the two very emotional women?" Yes, that would be us! Watching and sharing in the joy of other hikers as they completed their own journeys to the top of Katahdin concluded in a beautiful and fitting way the good fellowship that was experienced between AT hikers. Shaking hands in a congratulatory bond for we had each climbed our mountain; we had each fulfilled our individual vision...alone...together.

Conclusion

"Our truest life is when we are in dreams awake."
Thoreau

"If you don't risk anything, you risk even more."
Erica Jong

Hiking the entire Appalachian Trail was all I had dreamed of and so incredibly more than I could have ever envisioned. The AT changed my life! How those words lack so profoundly in articulate magnitude. For the changes it brought have touched me deeply with visible, applicable and enduring imprints physically, mentally, emotionally and spiritually. I am forever a different and better person than when I walked into the woods of God's Appalachian Mountains that leap day.

Physically, I learned a profundity of strength in

Walking my Dream!

myself that I never knew existed let alone trusted before. Feeling at times the most exquisite physical pain I have ever known, I continued to walk on, to live fully. I knew a level of fatigue unimaginable, but found a deep well of energy within me to tap. More importantly, regardless of the weariness and aches, I learned to even still appreciate the journey.

Along the way I realized anew and deeply that a gloomy day could be transformed into bright sunshine with an adjustment of psyche along with boot and pack straps. Attitude is everything! For mentally, the trail can certainly give you a ride up and down and sideways and back. Necessity instills a need to learn to balance and mellow this cycle to a more even and gentle traverse with the power in your mind, not your legs. The Talmud wisely speaks: "We do not see things as they are. We see them as we are." We are to say whether we find in the morning fog the mystery

Morning Fog on the Trail

of the deep woods or a disappointment in not being able to see farther. The "success" of a vision then, is really dependent on us – what we are and our perspective then on what we discover in that place. Inner and outer landscapes can certainly influence each other, taking their cues from one another, but we choose the title holder.

This experience heightened my awareness and

Happy "Scarf" on the Trail

heartfelt appreciation of so many things in life. I have always loved the out-of-doors, but being outside for an extended period of time – indeed months – taught me my own rhythms place in the natural world. Seasons and contrasts flowing one into the other created in me a resonating pulse with the natural world as well. Trees hugged me like a thick warm scarf. I learned the art of living simply – appreciating and celebrating the small gifts of life – clean water, simple food, rest, shelter, friends, sunshine, rain, wind, warmth and that splendid soft pillow. An aside here: when I got home from completing the trail many friends and family gave me tokens of congratulations. The two top recurring gifts were – yep, scarves and pillows! Simple joys enlarged my soul and made each day eloquent. My heart was given renewed trust in the basic goodness of human beings for I completed the Appalachian Trail not on my own, but with the continuous support and kindness of friends, family and strangers.

Even more so I was able to accomplish the AT through an inner strength that can only come from a higher power residing in me. Resonating within me where even the weather couldn't reach, was an inner tranquility. I felt, tangibly felt, God with me throughout this journey. A pure strength and an oh-so-gentle and loving pressure on my palm or

Maine Pond at Sunset

entwined in my fingers, feather soft, like that of a lover's caress on their beloved's cheek led me on. His might moved my legs when I couldn't and His heart beat fervently in mine. I had never grasped fully the warmth, steadfastness and power of God before. But on the trail, both perceptibly and energetically, His strength embodied my body, mind, heart and soul. His presence guided, powered, shared and helped me fulfill this journey. I was going to call my book, "God and Me and the AT." But I determined that wasn't so much a title- a descriptive heading - for my ramblings of words and feet, but an authorship- the source of my writing and success of my journey.

The passion living in a dream fulfilled is hard to express with a mere twenty six letters. There is, of course, an incredible deep residing personal satis- faction and awe that it is done. But what is done; what was I looking for in hiking the AT? In examining that question I realize I wasn't really searching for anything in this dream. I just wanted to walk thou- sands of miles across the mountains of Appalachia through the four seasons of our earth. But I did not walk 2000 miles. I walked one step. Then another and another. Such is anything in life that we dream and want to accomplish; we do it one step at a time. The vital point is to choose to do it! Significant also is to really be completely present with all your senses engaged when you are doing it. Then the ultimate aim is to then fully enjoy the doing!

In our modern society where goals of instant grat- ification drive many aspects of personal attitudes and governing policies, I feel many of us do not even enjoy the pleasure of the then-attained. We want it now, get it and then without even enjoying what we gained we immediately think of the next thing we want. We eat the ice cream cone mourning that the treat is gone on the first lick. We have the long-anticipated child then rush through their growing up, not noticing or gratifying in the precious single moments. We move finally into our new office without a second thought of enjoying the fresh space. We are not present in the now but are thinking of 5:00 PM or Friday and the weekend or vacation or when the kids are grown or when we are feeling better or when we have the money or the time.

Time - now that is our ultimate taskmaster in life and, not to be morbid, but death is each of our final "greatest mountain." So how dare we waste a moment of life time in our journey getting there! Live your life with presence, step by step, the pleasurable and the painful, each and every day, the small and the grand moments! Be there awake, living with gratefulness for each instant. As you undulate through your own individual journey, follow the white blazes that reside within you for they are there - known in your deepest mind, felt inside your beating heart and written on your very soul. Seize your days and live your dreams! Happy trails to you!

Guiding White Blaze